OPPORTUNITIES IN
BUSINESS
COMMUNICATION
CAREERS

Robert Deen

Foreword by
Norman G. Leaper, President
International Association of
Business Communicators

VGM Career Horizons
A Division of National Textbook Company
4255 West Touhy Avenue
Lincolnwood, Illinois 60646-1975 U.S.A.

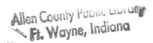

Cover Photo Credits

Front cover: upper left and right, lower left,
Amfac Distribution Corporation; lower
right, NTC.

Back cover: upper left, First National Bank of
Chicago; upper right, Republic Airlines; lower
left, Amfac Distribution Corporation; lower
right, NTC.

ABOUT THE AUTHOR

Robert Deen is Communications Manager for Amfac Distribution Corporation, one of the nation's largest wholesale distributors, with annual revenues exceeding $1.3 billion. He is responsible for the corporation's public relations and employee communications, and was formerly with an affiliate of Carl Byoir & Associates, the world's third largest public relations agency.

A graduate of Oregon State University with a B.S. in Technical Journalism, he holds a master's degree in Communications from California State University, Chico. His masters thesis, published in 1981, explored the relationship of the news media to community power structure theory.

A former public affairs officer for the United States Marine Corps, he worked as a PAO at the Marine Corps' largest base, Camp Pendleton, California. An honor graduate of the Department of Defense's Information Officer School, he served as the senior information officer for the 7th Marine Amphibious Brigade, the USMC component of the nation's Rapid Deployment Force. As a Marine lieutenant he also served as a platoon commander, combat engineer, and military parachutist/scuba diver.

He is active in a number of professional communications organizations, including the International Association of

Business Communicators, and played a key role in establishing a student chapter at California State University/-Chico.

Deen has been published in a variety of publications as a freelance writer and photographer, and makes a habit of maintaining contacts with the academic community and counseling students, recent graduates, and others considering business communications as a career.

FOREWORD

—A telecommunications company makes an important technological breakthrough and wants to announce it to the public and to potential investors.

—A hospital needs to alert doctors, nurses and administrative staff to new patient care schedules and visiting hours.

—A not-for-profit association decides to launch a public awareness campaign against drug abuse.

—A manufacturer needs to know how employees would feel about working in production teams.

—An industry association seeks to influence legislation affecting its products and services.

Today's business communicator is responsible for these and many other key activities. Where the communicator once focused on simply getting the company's message to employees via an in-house publication, now he or she prepares sophisticated messages for ever expanding and diversified audiences.

An estimated one-half million professionals in the U.S. and Canada manage and practice communication in such areas as government relations, public affairs, corporate communication, lobbying, fund-raising, marketing and promotion, community relations, labor relations, employee communication, media relations, advertising and many other related disciplines.

Depending on the nature and scope of the audience, duties may be as varied as managing a department of communication specialists, editing one or many publications, scriptwriting for corporate video news shows or training programs, speechwriting, preparing position papers, creating direct mail or advertising campaigns, conducting research and analyzing data, planning conventions and workshops, serving as a corporate advocate, leading executive training for media contact, and much, much more.

Business communication is changing and evolving. More than a third of those active in the profession today are in newly created positions, and the number of new jobs continues to increase rapidly.

These growing opportunities are bringing greater responsibilities and higher salaries to communicators. In the IABC Foundation's biennial "Profile" survey, over a third of the respondents said they had more significant roles in their organizations—and about 38 percent said management was giving greater support to communication.

One of the key roles these communicators play is in participating in planning and policy-making sessions to ensure that communication strategies are built into corporate plans and objectives. As the responsibilities have grown, salaries have increased significantly, too—rising in 1985 nearly 17 percent to an average of $33,900.

Business communication attracts thousands of new practitioners each year. With the range of available options, including organizations and managerial/technical skill areas, the profession offers opportunities for many.

This book provides the background and information you'll need to prepare for a career in business communication, a career most practitioners are blessed with. Two of three already in the field say they wouldn't change it for any other, and few do.

We hope this information will help you decide whether or not to become a business communicator. If you choose to do so, we welcome you to an exciting and rewarding profession.

Norman G. Leaper, ABC
President
International Association of Business Communicators

PREFACE

Communications is one of the fastest growing and most challenging career fields available, and its future is bright. In the years ahead there will be a growing need for businesses and organizations of all types to communicate with a wide variety of individuals and groups. Subsequently, there will be an increased need for skilled professionals to help make this happen, individuals able to take advantage of rapid advances in communication technologies.

In today's "information society," communications plays an important role, affecting the actions of organizations, the messages the public receives, and the ways in which it receives them.

This is a serious responsibility. Much of the future for communicators is uncharted ground. Communications professionals can expect growing status, increased financial and personal rewards, and an ability to claim a larger share of their organizations' resources.

In return, they will be expected to use their skills to produce significant, measurable results. They will be an important part of the management team, with the accompanying demands and responsibilities.

In short, business communications is a profession with a future, and an attractive profession for talented people who want to share in both the hard work and the rewards.

This book is not presented as a rigid guide to success. The profession is changing so rapidly that such a book would probably be obsolete before it came off the presses. What this book offers is assistance in entering the profession. It answers the questions you need—What do business communicators do? What skills do they need? How do they get those skills? Who do they work for, and where are the job opportunities?

Beyond that, it offers a practical guide to the process of seeking a position as a business communicator.

Like most things in life, your chance of eventual success in the field lies entirely in your own hands. The doors of opportunity are open. If this book can lend a helping hand in seizing those opportunities, then it was well worth the writing.

Robert Deen

ACKNOWLEDGMENTS

The author gratefully acknowledges the assistance of the following in the preparation of this book:

Norman G. Leaper, ABC, President, International Association of Business Communicators (IABC), and Clara Degen, IABC Vice President, Research/Education, and the members of the Sacramento, California chapter of the IABC, particularly Bruce Reid, Becky Moore, Betsy Stone, and Della Gilleran.

The faculty of the Department of Information and Communication Studies, California State University, Chico, and particularly John Sutthoff, Ph.D., Richard Ek, Ph.D., and Bob Vivian.

My wife Irene, and sons Aaron and Brian, for their moral support.

The author would also especially like to acknowledge Amfac Distribution Corporation and its management for providing an environment in which employees are encouraged to seek excellence both in performance and professional development.

CONTENTS

DEDICATION

To my mother and father, and to Dan Ocheltree, because real friends are few and far between.

Important business communications skills include the ability not only to write and edit company publications but also to create effective layouts. Photo: Amfac Distribution Corp.

CHAPTER 1

THE BUSINESS COMMUNICATION FIELD

WHAT IS BUSINESS COMMUNICATION?

There was a time when the attitude of many in the business community was, as Vanderbilt so pungently put it, "The public be damned." Business, government, and in fact most large organizations were largely insulated from public opinion. Information traveled slowly, mass communication had not truly developed, and the concept of "public opinion" had yet to jell.

That day is long past. In an increasingly complex and sophisticated society, organizations recognize that their continued success and existence depend largely on an ability to win the support and goodwill of various groups of individuals. These "publics" as they have been termed in the public relations field, may be external audiences —community members, customers, manufacturers, shareholders, or stockmarket investors. They may also be internal —employees, or the members of an organization such as a trade association.

Traditionally, public relations has been considered to be communication with external audiences for the purpose of influencing or persuading. "Business communicator" was

1

more likely a title for an individual concerned with internal audiences, most often the editor of an "in-house" publication for an organization.

Heavily influenced by new technologies, the "business communicator" today is increasingly an individual expected to be expert in communicating with both internal and external groups. As a staff function the communicator is the expert on communication techniques—using such techniques according to the goals and needs of the organization.

Communication According to Hay

According to the Hay Management Consultants, one of the nation's most respected communications and management consulting firms, no organization is forced to implement a formal communication system. Yet every organization has communication. It may be the grapevine (informal), memos, meetings, plan descriptions, etc.—in other words, every time an employee receives information about an organization communication has occurred.

As organizations have come to realize this, the question has become whether their communications are planned and controlled, or simply allowed to take place at random.

Communications is sometimes thought of in terms of a collection of presentations, articles, and media (slides, films, publications, etc.). Today, says Hay, it is much more. Communication is "the linking process that connects the organization's mission and its employee's activities. It is also the *only* way to transmit knowledge about goals, programs, or events." As such, communication is to be a management tool that sophisticated managers will use wisely.

Properly managed, communications efforts can be expected to produce clarity of direction (goals are understood), better understanding of job roles, credibility for top management, enhanced levels of employee knowledge, vehicles to obtain information, demonstrated commitment to employees, employee support, and precise performance expectations.

The Communication Model

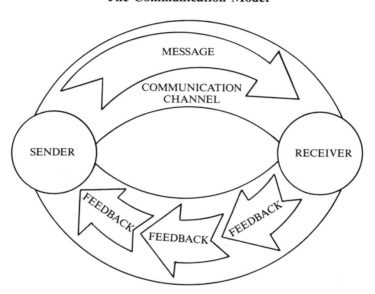

In its most basic description, communication involves three components: a sender, a message, and a receiver. A message is "sent" via a "communication channel" to the "receiver." Most models include "feedback," or acknowledgement that the message was received and understood.

Picture the organization as the sender. Every organization has goals and objectives. To achieve this it will need to communicate with internal or external groups. Perhaps it needs active support. Perhaps it merely needs lack of opposition. Communication is usually necessary to achieve either.

The role of the communicator is to help the organization identify its intended receiver (group, public or target audience), assist in shaping the message, and to identify or create the most effective communication channel to send the message.

To understand this better, consider two examples, one internal, one external.

Internal: A mid-sized business corporation has a problem: its costs for health care insurance are skyrocketing. Opinion research shows that the organization's employees are unnecessarily over-using medical benefits. Their attitude is "the insurance company pays the bills, so why not go to the doctor for every little thing."

The audience in this case is the corporation's non-management employees. The business communicator, in conjunction with management, decides that the message to be sent is, "the company pays for *every* health care dollar through self-insurance, and health care dollars are taking a growing slice of the limited benefit pie, keeping the company from spending on other benefits employees might desire more."

To send this message, the communicator may recommend:

- A series of feature articles on the issue in the company's in-house publication.
- A slideshow explaining how health care insurance works to be shown at employee meetings.
- Visually-oriented "payroll stuffers," or small flyers distributed in paycheck envelopes which explain the issue with illustrations, charts and pictures.

(In reality this would doubtlessly be an ongoing effort, but these might be the communicator's initial recommendations).

External: In this case, a company which sells drugs on a wholesale basis has developed new computer-based capabilities and consequently wants to move into new market areas. Where it formerly sold to small drug stores, it now wants to expand its business by selling to large hospital pharmacies. While the company's new computers give it the capability to serve this new market, it finds it has a credibility problem. Potential customers are leery of going with a company without an established track record in this new and more demanding field.

The audience in this case are pharmacy directors, and other hospital staff influential in the selection process. The business communicator, in conjunction with management, decides that the message will be "that the company's new computer capabilities, combined with an established history of service in the drug wholesaling industry, provide a unique capability to service hospitals."

The communicator recommends a public relations thrust to get publications read by the target audience to run stories about the company and its capabilities. Exhibits displaying the company's capabilities might also be set up at trade shows serving the hospital industry. The communicator may institute a continuing program of news releases highlighting each new hospital pharmacy customer to sign on with the company.

As these two examples demonstrate, communications has become an increasingly important tool for organizations to use in achieving their objectives. The function is not limited to "business" in the sense of corporate entities. Government, associations, non-profit groups, hospitals, banks, utilities, universities—virtually all organizations have discovered a need to communicate effectively and are staffed accordingly.

What can communications do for an organization? It can inform and educate, it can persuade, and it can motivate.

Ultimately, its goal is to influence human behavior. All organizations have human needs: a business needs productive workers; a university needs alumni who support it financially; a political party needs votes; a charity needs volunteers; a new restaurant needs customers. The list is endless. One of the greatest organizational innovations of this century is the recognition of the importance of proper communications, and the rise of professional communicators equipped to manage these efforts.

Generalist vs. Specialist

Within the business communications field, there are many sub-specialists—careerists in their own right. These individuals are expert in such areas as graphic design, photography, speechwriting, technical writing, copywriting, audiovisual production, instructional technology, editing, direct mail, electronic publishing, and market or opinion research. They play an important role in the overall communications process.

In communications management, on the other hand, an individual is expected to be knowledgeable, if not expert, in all communication areas, in order to successfully plan and direct the work of specialists.

Essentially it is a personal decision whether to construct a career as a specialist or to move into management. For some, management is a challenge and a natural direction of growth. For others it may only mean less time working in the area of expertise which they enjoy and do best.

Because the field is becoming increasingly complex and demanding, there will be a growing need for both the generalists who can understand and use the communications techniques available, and the specialists who are the complete masters of their areas of expertise.

HISTORICAL PERSPECTIVE

Communication for the purpose of influencing opinion and behavior is far from a new phenomenon. The Greeks and Romans addressed the influencing of public opinion (*Vox populi, Vox Dei:* The voice of the people is the voice of God). Machiavelli noted that "not without reason is the voice of the people compared to the voice of God." The word "propaganda" has a seventeenth century origin dating to the Catholic Church's establishment of the College of Propaganda to propagate the Roman Catholic religion.

America's birth was largely the result of expert "communicators" such as Samuel Adams and Thomas Paine, whose inflammatory writings helped bring the colonies to the point of revolution.

"Press-agentry," the pursuit of publicity for its own sake, became an American phenomenon, exemplified by circus showman P.T. Barnum and his "Greatest Show on Earth." It was George Creel's "Committee on Public Information" during World War I which, in the words of Edward Bernays (often called the founder of the field of public relations), "opened the eyes of the intelligent few in all departments of life to the possibilities of regimenting the public mind."

"Regimenting the public mind" is not the goal of today's business communicator. The practitioner today seeks to educate, to inform, to motivate, and to persuade. Successfully achieving this in our increasingly complex world depends upon the skillful use of a growing arsenal of sophisticated communication tools and techniques.

Organizations have responded to this need with professional communicators capable of understanding and reaching the many groups important to organizational success. Far from the days of "the public be damned," today's organizations and societal institutions are held accountable by the public—the public considers them responsible to society and open to examination—with the news media often the investigators. Communication has, in short, become a necessity; some would say a responsibility, and the professional business communicator has become one of the business world's most rapidly growing career areas as a result.

THE FUTURE

Three trends ensure the future need for professional communicators and at the same time place demanding challenges upon the men and women who will fill these roles. These trends are in large part responsible for the importance placed upon communications today, and will be a major part in shaping the future role of the professional communicator.

The first is the growing complexity of society. Far from the simple agrarian nation of the past, America today is a dynamic mixture of social, economic, and political forces. An individual is today a member of many "publics." Your neighbor might be a Democrat, a Catholic, a Rotarian, a small business owner, and a member of the PTA, a credit union, the National Rifle Association and the Chamber of Commerce. How many organizations do you belong to, or have an interest in? Would you consider yourself a part of the "public" of the local government, police department, hospitals, educational institutions, businesses, and political parties?

In an increasingly compartmentalized and specialized society, the need for communication between individuals and organizations will continue to grow correspondingly.

Another significant trend is the impact of technology, which seems to be outrunning the average individual's ability to understand and cope with the rapid rate of change. There is today, and will continue to be into the foreseeable future, a need for men and women with communication skills to help explain the impact of change and new technologies on our everyday lives. To ensure their continued success, organizations seeking to exploit or create change must communicate with the public to gain understanding and support.

A third trend is the advent of the "information society," in which information itself has become a form of power. This encompasses the realm of the computer and Management Information Systems—the management of information. The information society places greater power in the hands of the relative few who can control and manipulate information. In a free society, the role of the professional communicator may be that of the translator or interpreter, bridging the understanding gap between the computer-oriented managers of information and the public which needs to be an informed participant in the process.

SUMMARY

The communications process in its most basic form involves the sending of a message from a source to a receiver via a communication channel. In today's society, all organizations need to communicate with various audiences or "publics" to successfully achieve their organizational goals and objectives. The professional communicator's responsibility is to work with management to target audiences and shape appropriate messages, identify or create effective

The "statistically average" business communicator is a woman in her thirties and the manager of a corporate communications department. Photo: Amfac Distribution Corp.

communication channels, and to measure feedback—the audience's reception and level of understanding.

The increasingly specialized socioeconomic environment presents a real need not just to take message A and send it to audience B, but to shape and present that message in a fashion which is both easily understood and persuasive— affecting human behavior in a way consistent with the successful accomplishment of an organization's objectives.

That is both the challenge and the opportunity of the professional business communicator in the years ahead.

CHAPTER 2

THE BUSINESS COMMUNICATOR

Effective business communicators will need to know more about their business, about the marketplace and about the world around them than ever before, according to Irving Shapiro, former chief executive officer of E.I. duPont de Nemours and Company. "You must know the territory if you want to be helpful and effective."

James Bere, chairman and chief executive officer of Borg-Warner Corporation, adds that, "The day is over when communication dealt mainly with emergencies and scheduled routine. From now on, we will demand the same strategic plans from communicators that we expect from production and marketing and research—plans based on where the company wants to be in the years ahead, what it needs to get there and what the communication function can do to help."

Along with a greater emphasis on communication, according to John Bailey, a former president of the International Association of Business Communicators, has come a change in management style from the school of "tell 'em as little as possible but be firm about it" to an approach of genuine respect for the ever-changing, multi-faceted audience—an audience that seeks information, not commands.

Clearly, the communications function in today's organizational environment is one recognized as increasingly important. The business communicators who will manage this growing responsibility will need special skills and talents to succeed in a demanding and important career field.

THE BUSINESS COMMUNICATOR TODAY

What kind of people are business communicators? What kind of work do they do? What are their titles? How much do they earn?

The International Association of Business Communicators, in a survey of its 10,000 plus members, came up with a "statistically average" business communicator.

> A woman, she is 34 years of age and the manager of a corporate communication department in the finance and banking field where she spends at least 25 percent of her time on management functions, including the supervision of at least one employee. She has been in the field eight years, with her current employer four years, and in her current job at least two years. She earns $29,608.*

In addition, the typical communicator is a college graduate with a degree in journalism. She majored in the news editorial sequence while in college and entered the field from school, or spent two years on a newspaper before switching professions.

Her communications activities are most likely directed to employees, followed by management and administrators, and customers. Her messages address employee morale and motivation, cost containment, economic competition or productivity.

------

*All monetary amounts in this book are stated in U.S. dollars, unless otherwise noted.

Although she's satisfied with the profession, she's less satisfied with her organization and current job. She plans to stay on the job for the time being but expects to be with another organization within three to five years.

The Public Relations Society of America's "average" member, on the other hand, is male, works in corporate communications, is 41, majored in journalism, and earns $35,000 a year.

The IABC provides the following statistical profile of its membership:

AGE (median—34 years)

Under 30 years	21.6%
30-39 years	51.3%
40-49 years	16.6%
50-59 years	8.1%
60 years or older	2.4%

EXPERIENCE (median—8 years)

0-2 years	10.3%
3-4 years	13.9%
5-9 years	34.4%
10 years or more	41.4%

YEARS WITH ORGANIZATION (median—4 years)

0-2 years	31.9%
3-4 years	21.5%
5-6 years	17.3%
7-10 years	15.9%
11 years or more	13.4%

Information provided by organizations such as the IABC and PRSA, which represent a substantial percentage of America's professional communicators, offers insight into the profession today and its employment potential in the United States.

WHERE COMMUNICATORS WORK

Members of the IABC were distributed among the following employers in 1985:

Corporate	49.0%
Not-For-Profit	12.5%
Financial Institution	8.4%
Hospital/Medical	5.8%
Educational Institution	5.1%
Counseling Firms	4.5%
Government	4.5%
Self-Employed	6.0%

PRSA's members were employed in these areas:

Corporate	35%
Counseling Firms	21%
Not-For-Profit	12%
Education	7%
Health Care	6%
Government/Military	5%
Utilities	5%
Freelance Consultants	5%

Nearly one in four IABC members worked in a communication department in 1985. Areas of responsibility were:

Communication	23.8%
Public Relations	18.6%
Marketing/Advertising	10.6%
Internal Communications	6.8%
Personnel	6.4%
Corporate Relations	5.4%
Public Affairs	4.7%
Public Information	2.8%
Community Relations	1.9%
Administration	1.7%
Video AV	0.2%
Other	11.8%

Public Relations Society of America members defined their responsibility areas as:

Senior Managers	20%
Managers in Counseling Firms	27%
Middle Managers for PR Programs	31%
Media Relations	24%
Researchers, Writers	22%
Publications	13%

More than 37 percent of the IABC's members in 1985 were in newly created positions, while another 15.3 percent said they had replaced individuals promoted or transferred elsewhere.

About one in five replaced an individual who moved on to another organization and 5.4 percent moved into a vacancy created by retirement or death.

Nearly four of 10 communicators said they held the title of manager or director and just under 17 percent said they were editors. Five percent carry the title of vice president and 1.4 percent work freelance.

About two-thirds supervise a staff of eight, including communication professionals, secretarial, clerical and other employees. The number of employees under the communicator's direction ranges from one to 300, and the number of communication professionals averages five, with the range from one to 90.

Job satisfaction continues to rank as the most important job factor for nine out of 10 communicators. Next in importance, although at some distance, are creative opportunity, job freedom, adequate salary and professional development. Of lesser importance were promotion potential, managerial responsibility, job security and recognition by colleagues. Least important in the survey was prestige of position.

Nearly two in three communicators said they were satisfied

with the communication profession, 64.4 percent, while a mere 3 percent were dissatisfied with the profession.

Fewer than half said they were extremely or very satisfied with the organization for which they worked. Over 13 percent were dissatisfied with their employers.

Part of this dissatisfaction might be attributed to the fact that 16 percent see little or no support for public relations in their organization and nearly one-third feel they have a below average or poor chance for advancement.

However nearly half said their management's support for public relations was outstanding or above average and about 18 percent said their chances for advancement were above average or better.

Almost half the communicators surveyed expect to stay in their current positions for the time being, and nearly a third expect to be with their current employers in three to five years.

About 16 percent are currently job seeking and nearly 3 percent plan to start their own businesses in the near future.

SALARIES

During the two year period between the IABC's 1983 and 1985 surveys, salaries for organizational communicators increased nearly 17 percent to $33,900. Males continued to earn substantially more than women, averaging $40,773 to $29,608. However, women's salaries increased at a faster rate: 19.4 percent for women versus 15.8 percent for men.

Salaries ranged from a low of $10,000 reported by one practitioner, to a high of up to $99,999 reported by 15. The largest category of members, 36.8 percent, said they earned between $20,000 and $29,999.

When compared to educational levels, communicators with doctoral degrees earned the highest average salary, $39,589, followed by those with master's degrees, $38,589. Communicators with high school diplomas were at $32,508, topping salaries earned by college graduates, $31,465. Those with some post-graduate work earned $35,128.

Salary Distribution

$10,000—$12,499	0.7%
$12,500—$14,999	1.1%
$15,000—$17,499	4.9%
$17,500—$19,999	4.2%
$20,000—$29,999	36.8%
$30,000—$39,999	27.1%
$40,000—$49,999	13.2%
$50,000 or more	12.0%

EDUCATION

Nine out of ten business communicators are college graduates, with eight percent having at least some college or university credit. Less than two percent entered the profession with a high school diploma.

The number of communicators with higher degrees continues to increase. Those earning master's degrees increased 10.6 percent between IABC surveys, from 19.7 percent to 21.8 percent. The number of those with doctoral degrees is now 1.6 percent. Women are nearly twice as likely as men to have earned a bachelor's degree, 26.9 percent to 14.9 percent, a master's degree, 15.2 percent to 9.1 percent, or a doctoral degree, 13 percent to 8.8 percent.

Most communicators major in journalism, especially news/editorial sequences. Nearly one in five holds a degree in English or speech. Public relations specialties were the choice of 13 percent.

Education

High school	1.6%
Some college/university	8.1%
College degree	41.9%
Some post-graduate work	24.3%
Master's degree	21.8%
Doctoral degree	1.6%
Other	0.5%

HOW COMMUNICATORS ENTERED THE FIELD

Most business communicators took their first position in the field immediately after leaving school (27.6%) or after a short stint with a newspaper (19.1%). The majority were in a communication job within two years of college graduation.

About a third of the IABC's members say their formal education was excellent or very good in preparing them for their current jobs. Only 5.6% said their training was poor.

FUTURE EMPLOYMENT OUTLOOK

Probably the most telling of all statistics to emerge from the IABC's most recent annual membership survey was that nearly a third of those surveyed held newly created jobs. That fact is startling proof of a continuing growth trend in the field, with an ever increasing number of organizations demonstrating their appreciation of the communications function through higher communication budgets, larger communication staffs, and higher salaries for communications professionals.

All indications are that this trend will continue unabated into the foreseeable future, with employment and advancement prospects excellent for qualified business communication professionals and new entrants into the field.

IS BUSINESS COMMUNICATION
RIGHT FOR YOU?

Some people seem to instinctively and immediately know what career is right for them. Others agonize over the decision, or shift from job to job, never settling into a steady course. Choosing a career is one of the most important decisions anyone can make, and despite the hundreds of guidance books and employment counselors, it's a decision you ultimately must make for yourself. Chuck Yeager, the first pilot to break the sound barrier, once said that if you really loved doing something you were going to be good at it. Most people would agree, yet it's amazing how many people grind away at a job they hate. Perhaps there are exceptions; but for most of us to be a success in the long run, we have to enjoy what we're doing.

Is business communications for you? A high percentage of the people in the field are satisfied with their jobs. It's a growing field, one with opportunities, which lets you use your creativity, work independently, and grow to a level of responsibility you're comfortable with. Often the communicator has a great deal of control over her or his job, enjoys the respect of other workers, and can clearly see a significant contribution to the organization resulting from the work done.

Business communications can be stressful. It is a "high profile" job. When you do a good job, people see it. When you make a mistake, everyone knows about it. Because the work often involves the news media or large circulation publications, mistakes can be painful. It comes with the territory. And *everyone* makes mistakes, sooner or later. If you can't accept that eventuality, then you may want to choose a "safer" career. The other side of the coin is that in such a high visibility environment the person who performs will be recognized and move ahead.

Generally speaking, communicators must work well with others, and most say they enjoy working with people. That doesn't mean being a social butterfly, but unquestionably human relations is a big part of the job. There isn't a "perfect personality" for the job. Skills are more important than personality, and skills can be learned.

Skills

The job is communication, and that usually comes in three parts: shaping the message, defining the audience the message will go to, and creating the communication channel that will be used. If you're a specialist, such as a speech writer, you'll work exclusively with that medium. If you're a generalist, or involved in management, you'll be expected to be familiar with an ever-widening variety of communication tools and able to recommend the most effective and efficient one for a particular use.

What sort of communication channels and skills are involved? Writing is the most predominant, and is a prerequisite for working in the field. And there are different types of writing: technical writing, speech writing, news writing, feature writing, advertising copywriting, writing for direct mail, and more. Versatility is important, unless your career decision is to specialize.

If you work with publications, besides writing you'll need editing skills, and layout and design knowledge. You may need to be a competent public speaker, to be able to manage and work with other people, or plan and organize events and activities. You may conduct opinion research, or evaluate other's research.

Typical projects a communicator might be involved in include newsletters, slideshows, videotapes, speechwriting, speakers bureaus, direct mail, news releases, brochures, annual reports, media relations activities, readership surveys, displays, posters, and producing in-house publications.

Evaluating Yourself and Focusing on Goals

Do you have what it takes to be a business communicator? The answer is probably yes, if you want it. That's true for most careers. If you want to be something, you can acquire the skills to be a success. The next chapter focuses on ways to acquire business communication skills.

The important thing—and it isn't as easy as it sounds—is to focus on your career goals. Say to yourself, "This is what I want to be, to achieve," and then go out and do it. There isn't any other way. Intelligence and natural talent count for a lot, but determination is the real key. You can do it.

Students at the University of Virginia's Colgate Darden Graduate School of Business Administration review cases together. Photo: University of Virginia, Gary Alter, photographer.

CHAPTER 3

ACQUIRING THE SKILLS: EDUCATION AND TRAINING

Information serves as fuel for the human mind. Whether it is fuel that burns hot and clean and powers productive movement or the kind that burns unevenly and clogs the system is another question.

Norman Nager and T. Harrell Allen
Public Relations Management by Objectives

How do you acquire the skills to become a professional communicator? Or, if you've made a start in the field, how do you keep learning and growing in a way that will help you move up the career ladder?

The answer lies of course in a combination of many elements. Education, both undergraduate and graduate, plays an important part. Membership in professional organizations, professional development seminars, internships, continuing education, and selective on-the-job training are other options. After focusing on a career objective, you must pick and choose from among many different options to develop the appropriate skills and make the best use of that most valuable of resources—your own time.

WHAT SKILLS ARE NEEDED?

The skills used in the business communications profession are many and varied. This fact emphasizes the importance of focusing on your employment objectives in order to acquire the necessary skills and experience.

In a recent survey of the members of the International Association of Business Communicators the following skill areas were identified as those most commonly used by the membership:

Communication theory	News writing
Feature writing	Newsletter editing
Magazine layout	Photography
Graphic design	Scriptwriting
Speakers bureaus	Government relations
Event planning	Management skills
Media contact	Budgeting/cost control
Personnel supervision	Audience research
Feedback systems	Communication planning
Investor relations	Audiovisual production
Speech writing	Proposal writing
Identity programs	Time management
Film production	Print production

EDUCATION

Communications has been a "hot" field of undergraduate education in the United States, with communications schools and departments expanding even as overall enrollment dropped at many institutions during the 1980's. Majors in public relations, communications, journalism, and related areas are offered at most major universities today.

Choosing the right university and the right program is not an easy task however. The field has grown so rapidly, and is new in so many aspects, that programs vary tremendously from institution to institution. This makes it all the more important to identify employment objectives early to make educational choices more meaningful. Once your objective is focused, shop carefully and ask the following questions:

What is the scope of the program offered? Does communications receive priority within the institution's overall program, or is the department a small "add-on" which may not receive its fair share of resources?

Is the department's curriculum oriented toward practical skills, theory, or a balance of both? What suits your needs best?

Do instructors have "real world" experience in the field? Have they been published on the subject? Are they involved in research? Will they have the time—and inclination—to help on a one-to-one basis? Do they stay in touch with professionals in the field, professionals who might provide valuable job leads for you after graduation?

What is the program's reputation among professional communicators? As potential employers, that reputation may affect your future job search.

Does the institution offer access to the latest technology, such as word processing, personal computers, electronic publishing, and video production? The trend in business is clearly towards automation, and graduates proficient with electronics and the latest technologies will have an edge.

Facilities at the University of Miami's School of Communications, for example, include a cable television studio, a 24-hour cable channel, film and video equipment, still-photography studios, a 300-seat motion-picture house, film studios, a computer-equipped editing lab, a graphics lab, and an electronic bulletin board.

GENERALIST OR SPECIALIST?

Well-defined career objectives help you decide how to best use your educational experience. One decision which must be made is whether to seek a broad-based, general communications education which exposes the student to the widest possible selection of knowledge and skills, or to focus on one particular area of expertise to learn as much about it as possible.

If your goal is to be a multi-faceted business communicator who will eventually move into a communications management position, then you will probably choose the generalist route. If, on the other hand, your goal is to become a specialist in communications graphics, an audiovisual producer, or a technical writer, then you will want to focus your educational experience accordingly.

Another decision will be whether to emphasize hands-on, practical learning that teaches skills directly applicable to an entry-level job—writing, layout, production—or expand your background in communications theory, public relations strategy and planning, or the exposure to economics, sociology and psychology professional "persuaders" find useful. Probably a mix of both is wise, but again the choice should be carefully tied to career objectives.

INTERNSHIPS

Internship programs are proving to be an increasingly popular way for students to gain hands-on experience in their field of study while earning university credit at the same time. Many universities have well-developed contacts with businesses across the country for placing students in temporary working situations.

Many educators view internships as a "bridge" between the working world and the academic environment, with the student working in a business situation under the supervision of professional communicators. Businesses view internships as opportunities to develop new talent, with many interns being offered employment after graduation.

The communications internship program at California State University, Chico, for example, offers internships in the areas of radio, television, graphics, public relations, print and instructional technology. Organizations which participated in the most recent year included the California Beef Council, Capitol News Service, Dailey & Associates (San Francisco), International Business Communications (Washington, D.C.), KGO-TV (San Francisco), KNTV (San Jose), Los Angeles Magazine, Pacific Educational Network (San Francisco), Sacramento Magazine, Sun Diamond Corporation, Whitney Education Service, and the Wine Institute (San Francisco).

"It was like a first job," according to Linda Cassell, a recent participant in the CSU Chico program. "I feel a lot more confident as an individual and I feel a lot more confident in the field of communications. Coming back to school, I feel like I know what I need to get from my classes, and what areas I need to push myself in."

Student-run public relations "companies" are one of the latest developments in the trend to gain practical experience while in school. Frank Walsh, course sequence head of public relations at the University of Texas at Austin, recently explained in *P.R. Journal* magazine that "Our students literally set up an agency. They have an office, choose directors and account executives, seek clients and enter into contractual arrangements. They are paid for their services and the emphasis is on practical experience."

Most "clients" are not-for-profit organizations with small

public relations budgets. Typical tasks include writing newsletters and pamphlets, covering special events for the local news media, producing media kits, arranging press conferences and media placement.

GRADUATE STUDY

Graduate study is becoming an increasingly popular option among professional communicators. An advanced degree can provide greater expertise in communications theory, research and practice. Possession of a degree can lend personal credibility to the practitioner, who must often deal with senior management—invariably older, more seasoned and often skeptical.

Many communications professionals are opting for Master of Business Administration degrees, which they feel provide better grounding for success in the business environment.

Undergraduate students often face the choice of immediately pursuing an advanced degree following graduation, or entering the job market and returning later for graduate work. While this is a personal decision which will depend upon individual goals, most practicing communications professionals recommend the latter course.

As with undergraduate programs, the choice of a graduate program should be a careful, well-researched one, and many of the same questions should be asked.

SCHOLARSHIPS

Many communications-oriented scholarships are available to students. These may be offered by communications departments, professional communications organizations, businesses, institutions or individuals. Information can be obtained directly from these organizations, from communications instructors, or from financial aid departments.

Scholarships offer not only financial assistance, but look good on resumes and may help develop contacts useful in later job searches.

PROFESSIONAL DEVELOPMENT

The practicing communications professional never learns everything there is to know about the field, if for no other reason than that it is a dynamic, constantly changing profession. Technological change alone constantly affects the communications function, at a seemingly frenetic pace.

The business communicator constantly seeks ways to learn about new trends, develop new skills and improve old ones. These include reading professional books, magazines and journals. It may mean taking advantage of professional seminars or returning to the university for evening classes. Or it may mean making a special effort to interact with other communicators to discuss new developments and techniques.

There are a number of professional organizations which specifically serve the need of the business communicator to continually update skills and knowledge. These include but are not limited to the International Association of Business Communicators and the Public Relations Society of America. While the benefits of participating in professional organizations are more fully discussed in Chapter 8, it is worth noting that most offer professional development courses and seminars, professional journals and books, conferences and speakers, and opportunities to meet with and discuss communications problems and developments with other practitioners.

JOB EXPERIENCE

Clearly the most common and best means of gaining professional communications skills is through job experience. There is no substitute for actually doing something. Sometimes the communicator will be asked to perform a job that requires skills which he or she may not be expert in. That is the nature of any job environment. In such a situation the professional researches the problem, perhaps seeks outside assistance, but in any event tackles it to the best of her or his ability. In the process we learn and better prepare ourselves for future assignments.

The most important aspect of job experience is that as much as possible the communicator should seek jobs which will provide the experience and skills necessary to move towards career objectives. If the ultimate career objective is to become a well-rounded, broadly experienced communications manager, then sticking with a single job in a narrow specialty would be unwise. The communicator should strive to move around within the organization or, if that is impossible, consider changing organizations as opportunities present themselves. On the other hand, the communicator who seeks to be a specialist in a given area would not want to spend too much time working in communications positions unrelated to that specialty.

SUMMARY

The skills needed to be a successful business communicator are many and varied. To ensure that your valuable and limited resources of time and money are best used, employment objectives should be defined and focused. Efforts should be concentrated on obtaining those skills necessary to be a success in the position sought.

Communications skills may be obtained in numerous ways. Most universities offer communications programs, with many offering advanced degrees. Institutions vary considerably in the nature and quality of instruction offered, so the choice of an educational program should be a carefully considered one. Ability of an educational institution to offer access to the latest in technology should be a major consideration, as should the quality and extent of internship programs.

Advanced degree programs are increasingly popular with business communicators, with many opting to return to school after having started their careers. Some choose to hone communications skills such as research and theory in Master of Arts programs, others polish their business credentials through MBA programs.

For the practicing professional, development of skills should be an ongoing process. Professional organizations are one of the best sources of support. Seminars, conferences, and professional reading provide valuable information.

The best source of all for developing skills is actual on-the-job experience. Choice of jobs, as much as possible, should be determined by development of the skills necessary to reach an individual's ultimate career objective.

Public information personnel for the American Red Cross use writing
and editing skills to produce many kinds of documents: brochures,
pamphlets, annual reports, grant applications. Photo: American Red
Cross, Memphis Area Chapter.

CHAPTER 4

EMPLOYMENT OPPORTUNITIES BY INDUSTRY SECTOR

People are always blaming their circumstances for what they are. I don't believe in circumstances. The people who get on in this world are the people who get up and look for the circumstances they want, and, if they can't find them, make them.

George Bernard Shaw
Mrs. Warren's Profession

Appreciation of the importance of good communication has reached an all-time high—not just in corporate boardrooms but in virtually all large organizations, no matter what their purpose. Never before, it seems, have organizations been so interested in communicating effectively and frequently with groups important to them—whether employees, customers, union members, the media, the local community, or any other of a huge number of "publics."

With this growing appreciation of the contribution of proper communications has come added responsibility and stature for the communications profession. No longer is the communications professional simply editor of the in-house publication. Today the role is more likely to be custodian of an organization's image, and manager of a communications program encompassing sophisticated audiovisual techniques, electronic publishing, opinion research, marketing support, issues management, and advanced public relations techniques. With growing responsibility has come an accelerated need for professionals expert in a broad range of technical and specialized fields. Challenges abound.

Opportunities in the field continue to expand as more and more organizations recognize the need for communications, and become willing to increase the resources devoted to the function. While the business communicator is most frequently associated with the corporate environment, in fact the profession is widespread in many other sectors of private industry, government, education, health care, and others.

CORPORATE COMMUNICATIONS

Corporate communications is often viewed as the "purist" field for the business communicator, featuring work within the corporate environment. The communicator is directly responsible for supporting business goals and objectives, and the position's value is preferably measured by demonstrated contribution to the bottom line. A corporate communicator is accountable, with rewards commensurate with success.

Corporate communicators can expect to be involved in a wide range of activities. As they first enter the field they will usually work in a well-defined area, such as employee or "internal" communications. Some may be technical experts, such as those producing audiovisual products, and indeed many choose to specialize in a given area, spending their entire careers as writers, producers, photographers, etc. Others destined for communications management are expected to obtain competency, if not expertness, in a wide range of areas. They must grasp a feel for the utility of various communications tools and techniques, at the same time gaining the experience and expertise to craft detailed communication strategies designed to meet specific goals and objectives.

A corporate communicator can expect heavy involvement in employee communications, public relations (external audiences), supporting marketing efforts, and production of various internal publications. Increasingly electronic publishing—the in-house production of materials via computer capabilities—is a part of the corporate communicator's job.

Employment opportunities will continue to be good in corporate communications in the years ahead. An individual who has identified a particular industry or field of interest will have no difficulty finding business organizations with communications needs.

WORKING WITH AN AGENCY

Outside agencies which provide expertise to business organizations have flourished in recent years. These range from the very large advertising and public relations agencies that are corporations in their own right, to the one or two person "shop" meeting organizational needs on a consulting basis.

In addition to advertising and public relations, agencies exist which provide advice and assistance in marketing, graphic design, publication production, and production of audiovisual materials. In fact most agencies are a mix of talent and capabilities tailored to meet the specific needs of the businesses they serve.

Working for an agency has a number of advantages. Because an agency deals with a wide range of clients, the diversity of experience and skills to be gained is considerable. A communicator will be faced with a continually changing array of problems, opportunities and solutions. This provides an excellent opportunity to build the wide range of skills necessary for advancement in the field.

Partly for this reason, agency experience is prized by employers seeking in-house communications staff, and it is a common experience for an agency member to be hired away by a client. In this sense, agency work is an excellent stepping stone for an individual targeting a corporate position, particularly if an agency serves the types of corporations and industries which the communicator has selected as the preferred area of employment.

Agency work also has the reputation for being fast-paced, exciting, and "glamorous." It also can be less secure, with staffs increased or decreased according to the work load. Loss of a key client can seriously affect an agency, particularly smaller ones. Entry level jobs may be scarce. Small agencies can offer little in formal training, with employees expected to pull their own weight virtually from the first day.

GOVERNMENT

Some observers may not immediately associate working for the government with "business" communications. In reality, the needs of large government organizations are very similar to those of a business, and individuals frequently move between the public and private sector during their careers. Employee communications is just as much a concern in the public as the private sector. Public relations is important too, although it is virtually never called public relations in the public sector. Public Information Officer is a common title.

In theory, PIOs are assigned the task of facilitating the

flow of information from a government organization to the public, fulfilling the public's right to know how its government is functioning and how the taxpayers' dollars are being spent. Critics will argue that PIOs often perform "public relations" duties, trying to given an organization the best possible image without regard to public responsibilities.

Controversy aside, there are roughly 100,000 separate units of government in the United States—federal legislative, executive and bureaucratic agencies; state, city and county governments, districts, and more. Communicators are found in virtually all of these, from the state park information officer to city PIOs to the well-paid communication chiefs of major federal agencies.

POLITICS

The public information office—an entrenched part of the governmental bureaucracy—should not be confused with the political communicator. Political campaigns are relatively brief (but intense). They rely heavily on communication techniques for success. They depend upon volunteers, and thereby offer an excellent opportunity for gaining experience. In many respects, political campaigning resembles advertising more than business communications—with emphasis on image over substance. Agencies exist which specialize in political campaigns, although they concentrate in major governmental and media centers, with opportunities scarce elsewhere.

Political communicators often become "press aides" to successful candidates. Experience in political communications also can lead to involvement in lobbying—the courting of the political process to obtain results in favor of a client. Public relations and communications techniques are increasingly being applied to influence the legislative process, with some agencies specializing in such work.

Corporate business communicators will often find themselves involved in "public affairs," loosely defined as using persuasive techniques (lobbying, public relations, public education) to influence the governmental/legislative process in favor of a business entity's objectives. Political experience can be very valuable to a business communicator seeking one of these positions—usually senior and well-paying.

THE ARMED FORCES

Many top business communicators received their start in the field as public affairs (or public information) officers for the nation's military. The services employ both civilians (civil service) and military personnel in these capacities. The concept of the military PIO is based on the right of the public to know how its defense dollars are being spent, how well the country is defended, and how the men and women serving the country are being trained and treated.

The military can be an excellent starting place for a newcomer to gain that sometimes illusive initial experience so necessary in securing employment. Not only does the military offer excellent communications training (the Defense Information School is located at Fort Benjamin Harrison, Indianapolis), but opportunities to gain real world experience are excellent. A junior officer can expect to be placed in a much greater level of responsibility than a recent college graduate in the private sector. Many employers prefer candidates with three or four years of military experience for this reason. The military also provides a good background in management and personnel training.

The typical military PIO will be assigned to a military installation in a public affairs office. This office will be responsible for internal communications (usually producing the base newspaper) and external communications (dealing with the news media). Community relations is also a big part of the PIO's job.

Typical assignments for an average day might include escorting news media persons as they view field training, making a luncheon presentation to a civilian organization from the local community, or drafting a message from the base commander to the men and women in uniform assigned to the base.

The four services, Army, Navy, Air Force and Marines, while similar in their public affairs functions are quite different overall. An individual should carefully explore each for the possibility of being guaranteed work in the public affairs field, possible assignment locations, and training available.

While the military can be a very good employment route for the right individual, it is a larger commitment than a regular job. In fact it is more a lifestyle than a job. Anyone considering joining the armed forces—for any type of position—should make the choice carefully. The bottom line goal of the services is to defend the country, and its members are asked to make a greater personal commitment and demonstrate a greater willingness to sacrifice than in all but a few civilian organizations.

NON-PROFIT ORGANIZATIONS

There are thousands of non-profit organizations which need professional communicators. Names like the Red Cross, United Way, YMCA, YWCA, PBS, JCC, American Lung Association, Boy Scouts and Girl Scouts come to mind. The list is long.

Because these organizations usually depend heavily (or entirely) on contributions, their communications staff is often oriented towards "development" or fundraising activities.

Working for non-profit organizations can be long on psychic reward—feeling good about working for a worthwhile cause. Typically, however, the positions do not pay well. But this in turn makes them a good opportunity for the entry level job seeker. The trade off for less pay is a chance to gain valuable experience, make contacts, build a portfolio, and enjoy meaningful work.

Since the non-profit organization can be anything from a very large national organization to a small local group, the range of positions and needs is great. Small groups may not even have paid staff, but offer a worthwhile avenue for volunteer work.

Working with a non-profit entity in a community is also an excellent way to meet the area's "movers and shakers"— the local power structure—and to make contacts in the business community which may pay off in upward mobility later on.

In addition to the usual communication skills, employers of non-profit organizations will be looking for someone who can work well with volunteers and produce results on a slim budget. This is demanding, challenging work for the communications professional. There are many who thrive on it.

ASSOCIATIONS

The world today is networked by the national and international activity of associations. There are thousands of these groupings of individuals with common interests. It seems everyone belongs to at least one, usually more. Associations represent people with common business interests, hobbies, backgrounds, ethnicity . . . the list seems endless.

Associations exist for many reasons. They provide information, and offer members an avenue to meet and communicate with one another. They may represent members' political interests—lobbying in the state or provincial capital or in Washington, D.C. or Ottawa, Ontario. They may be involved in marketing the product of the members, as in agricultural associations. They may create public relations programs to polish the image of the group or business sector they represent.

All of these associations must communicate on a regular and frequent basis with their members. They publish magazines and newsletters, produce audiovisual materials and hold conferences. They may communicate with outside groups, other associations, business leaders and politicians, or members of the news media and government officials.

To do all this associations need trained, professional communicators. The growth of associations clearly seems to be on the upswing, and opportunities for communicators appear destined to grow with them.

EDUCATION

There are two distinct areas of opportunity for business communicators in education. They may teach the profession (primarily at the college level), or they may represent an educational institution as a communications staff person.

Communications departments have generally flourished during recent years, even where enrollment has dropped in other academic disciplines. To some extent this reflects increased interest in degrees which promise a likelihood of employment. The actual structure of communication programs varies. Some schools offer degrees in public relations, communications, journalism, and other related areas. They may be combined departments or separate in and of themselves. At other schools, public relations may be taught in the business, communications, or journalism departments, or even at all three!

Teaching at the college level usually requires at least a master's degree, with a PhD. preferred. A doctorate is virtually mandatory for a tenured, career position, although part time positions can sometimes be combined with other jobs and look good on a resume as well.

In a sense, there are two avenues to academic positions: the individual who works his way up the academic ladder, and the individual who returns to teach after a career as a practitioner.

In addition to teaching, all large educational institutions and most small ones have communications staff. This is an area of opportunity business communicators should explore. School districts of all types, community colleges, private schools, universities, and vocational schools all need to communicate with their students, with prospective students, with parents, and with alumni. As institutions they have the same public relations, internal communications, and community relations needs as any other organization. Many educational institutions are indeed businesses, with all the needs for advertising, marketing and selling expertise that any large corporation has.

HEALTH CARE

Health care is a rapidly changing field. It is becoming more competitive, more cost-conscious, and more communications sensitive. Help-wanted ads for marketing professionals with health care experience are remarkably common.

Hospitals are found in nearly every community. Their need to communicate with the members of the community is great. This has become a fast growing field with numerous opportunities and financial rewards, and should be considered by anyone contemplating entering the field. Health care is *big business,* and is destined to become even bigger as the population grows older and people become more health conscious.

As the industry changes rapidly in the future—the result of new technologies, population shifts, economic realignments and political change—health care institutions will need to explain themselves and gain the understanding and support of the public. Professional communicators will be much in demand to help in this.

MISCELLANEOUS

The search for employment opportunities in the communications field seems limited only by individual imagination. Virtually every organization has communication needs. If the organization is not large enough to support communications staff, then it may seek to fill its needs through agencies or freelance assistance.

Other areas to explore include chambers of commerce, economic development organizations, real estate development firms, the news media (large newspapers have public relations staff and television stations have public affairs directors), convention centers and bureaus, and state fairs. Consider the financial community: banks, credit unions, and savings and loans. Hotels, restaurants, franchise chains—if it is a business it will have communication needs. Your task is to identify an industry in which you have an interest and for which you have skills and talents to offer.

Electronic publishing promises to change the way business
communication takes place. Photo: Apple Computers.

CHAPTER 5

EMPLOYMENT OPPORTUNITIES: SPECIALTIES

As a member of the management team, the business communicator is expected to be knowledgeable (if not expert) in a wide range of communications skills. The communications manager is expected to make sound judgments about the appropriateness and cost effectiveness of various communications options in obtaining desired results.

Most communication managers work as specialists early in their careers, gaining the necessary expertise and exposure to skill areas. At some point an opportunity presents itself, and a conscious decision is made to move into management. Perhaps early career paths are carefully charted to gain a broad exposure to the widest possible variety of communication skills—laying the groundwork for the eventual move into communications management.

Many communicators do not choose to go into management. Indeed, it is a difficult decision for most because it means leaving behind a particular skill or activity which may have been a primary source of pride and job enjoyment. Managers spend more time planning and "managing" than "doing."

Many people decide to remain in their primary area of expertise. Obviously, highly skilled specialists are an essential part of the communications function, and remaining a specialist does not necessarily mean a less rewarding career—whether measured by status, job satisfaction, or financial reward. It is, however, a personal decision.

There are a wide range of specialties which any prospective business communicator will want to consider, either as a career or as a step in broadening one's base of experience and expertise.

WRITING SPECIALTIES

Speech Writing

While prominent in the political arena, speech writing is a function found in most large organizations. Specializing in a particularly demanding writing form, skilled speech writers command hefty salaries and can exert considerable influence in some major policy decisions.

There is more to speech writing than simple writing ability. Subject-area research, audience analysis, use of rhetorical structure, and a knack for writing words which will be spoken rather than read are all key elements.

In organizations which are not large enough to support a full time speech writer, this responsibility often falls to the senior individual responsible for communications.

Newswriting

Competency in journalistic writing or "newswriting," is expected of virtually all business communicators. While this work may sometimes be assigned to a beginner, newswriting demands well-developed skills and can't be taken lightly. A business communicator must have clearly established capability in newswriting to advance in the profession.

Newswriting may involve writing for internal publications, or the drafting of news releases for public relations purposes.

Most journalists are critical of the quality of news releases (unfortunately all too often with good reason), and would argue about calling public relations writing "newswriting." There's merit in that because the two are different. The point here, however, is that topnotch professional communicators understand the definition of news, know how to gather information, and can put it into the journalistic format—whether in a newsletter story or a news release. This is one reason why many business communicators are recruited from the ranks of journalism.

Occasionally a newswriting task will be a part of an employment application test, because the ability is viewed as a prerequisite to working in the business communications field.

As a specialty in business communication, newswriting is somewhat limited in career terms; it is an ability which is expected of all career communicators. The serious writer might wish to consider a career in journalism, where writing could be the major focus of a long term career. Another alternative might be to consider freelance writing, which is discussed in Chapter 9.

Feature Writing

Feature writing differs from newswriting in that it involves "soft" news, or items of human interest with less of a time element.

A story about an employee receiving an award might be "straight" news, for example, while an article about an employee's hobby of repairing bicycles to give to needy children at Christmas would be a feature.

Top quality feature writing is all too rare and a flair for it is a definite asset. Also, the format offers more room for creativity and self-expression than the "formula" structure of newswriting.

As a career specialty, feature writing is fairly limited. A large organization or agency might have writers specializing in features, but it is more likely to be a part of a broader writing position. Demonstrated skill in the area can be a big plus in a portfolio, however.

Technical Writing

Technical writing is a new, high growth communications specialty. It requires both writing ability and an ability to understand and work with technical subjects, particularly computer hardware and software fields.

The technical writer is often the intermediate in the communication process between engineer and final user, and must translate the engineer's often technical communications into user "documentation," or usage explanations, which will be clear, concise, and easily understood by the non-expert.

Technical writers often work with a marketing staff to produce materials which both "sell" a technical product and explain how it works and is used.

There has been a high demand in recent years for specialist writers of this type and consequently salaries have been good in comparison with many other writers, particularly at the entry level. Given the growth of "high technology" products and organizations, the prospects in this area appear very good for the future.

Script Writing

Script writing belongs in the audiovisual production/ instructional technology realm. Writing "for the ear", or to be spoken aloud rather than read, is a markedly different task than "print" writing. Some communicators are able to do both well.

Script writing requires a consciousness of the mix with a visual medium, and usually a good knowledge of the technical processes involved in audiovisual production. This is an area where turning to a specialist is often the best course of action, and the market for specialists is good. Because audiovisuals such as slide shows, films and videotapes have many organizational and business uses, the script writer may work on marketing projects, employee communications, public relations, or training programs.

Freelancing

Freelance writing is a description of the business arrangement under which writing is done, rather than a style of writing. Basically it describes writing on a contract or outside agreement for an organization rather than as an employee.

This area of writing is covered in detail in Chapter 9.

OTHER COMMUNICATION SPECIALTIES

Graphic Design

Graphic design is the actual construction of visual communication "packages," such as brochures, newsletters, annual reports, flyers, packaging, advertisements, logos, and stationery. Traditionally, the graphic designer uses typeset copy, photographs, illustrations, and other graphic devices to combine into a finished product.

Where the writer uses words, the graphic designer uses visual symbols, graphic devices, and layout techniques to communicate. High quality "print" pieces usually require a writing/design "team" able to work in concert. Where one or the other is neglected, the balance is lost and the product suffers.

While this is certainly not a rule, it is uncommon to find an individual with a high level of expertise in both areas.

Graphic designers may work as a part of an organization's in-house communications, advertising or marketing function, or in an agency environment.

A related and growing area is the creation of computer generated graphics, as well as graphic design via computer capabilities, as in electronic publishing.

Photography

Most photography is done by specialists, despite the fact that most in-house business communicators are competent photojournalists—that is, competent to take "news" photographs of reproduction quality. However, high quality photography is not the result of casual efforts, and requires professional techniques and equipment.

Photography is a large field with many opportunities; and while it is clearly a part of the business communications function, it is not an area that would lead readily to a management career path. Like many areas that are extremely specialized, it lacks broad exposure to other skill areas. It is also an area with many sub-areas of specialization, and can lead into other fields unrelated to business communications.

There are many career opportunities for photographers in business communications however, as in-house staff, with agencies, or on a freelance basis. As a skill, it is something every communicator should be comfortable working with, whether in creating the photographs or using them as a standard communication tool.

Audiovisual Production

The use of audiovisuals in public relations, advertising, marketing, training, and internal communication continues to grow. More and more organizations are discovering the impact and effectiveness of the audiovisual medium. There will be a growing need for skilled technicians to work in this field in the future.

The term "audiovisual" can apply to a variety of media, including film, videotape, and slide shows. Large organizations maintain internal audiovisual capabilities. Smaller operations often rely on outside producers to meet their needs.

An individual responsible for audiovisual production might be required to evaluate a communications problem and the audiences involved, select the proper audiovisual medium, research and write the script, outline the visuals in advance, supervise the filming or photography, and oversee the editing process which creates a final product.

Instructional Technology

Closely allied to audiovisual production, instruction technology is a new field focusing on the use of various technologies—many audiovisual—for training or instructional purposes.

This area is very specialized and may not be viewed as closely allied with traditional business communications. For career purposes, it would be advantageous to have a knowledge of the field without necessarily working it it. For individuals with an interest, however, it can be a rewarding career specialty.

Advertising

Advertising as a career field is not necessarily a part of, or identical to, business communications. Its emphasis is on persuasive techniques designed to reach external audiences through paid medium messages. However, the functions are close enough that inevitably the business communicator will be either involved with advertising efforts, or at least coordinating communication efforts with advertising campaigns. For this reason a knowledge of advertising is advantageous, and experience in the field can be useful; but advertising is a distinct career area in its own right, albeit one closely allied with business communications.

Marketing Communications

Marketing communications as a function is closely related to advertising. Essentially it is concerned with communications channels which support the marketing, or sale, of an organization's products or services. This can vary considerably according to the industry or organizational purpose, but might include such communication tools as direct mail, advertising, point of sale displays, trade show exhibits, and special sales promotions.

Marketing research is a highly specialized field which may be designated a part of marketing communications, and public relations often involves marketing support.

In certain sectors of the economy—most notably the health care industry—marketing has taken on increased importance in recent years. As a growing part of the business communications field, many talented individuals have made lateral moves into this specialty to take advantage of new opportunities.

Internal/Employee Communications

For many years the term "business communicator" was associated with being the editor of the organization's in-house publication. Internal communications was *the* focus of the field. While this is no longer strictly the case, internal communications remains a major concern and working area of business communications. It may be one of many responsibilities an individual may have, or it may be a specialty. Larger organizations with large numbers of employees usually have positions dedicated to this function.

It is a broad area. Paralleling the general definition of a business communicator, the audiences are those considered internal—employees, retirees, mid-management, senior management, and perhaps shareholders. The responsibility is to help management define and shape its messages for these audiences, then recommend or create the most effective and cost-efficient communication channel to deliver the message.

Communicating with employees is recognized as being of increasing importance to organizations today. Its quality, or lack thereof, can make a significant, measurable impact on a company's bottom line. It can play a key role in keeping highly qualified and needed employees. It can help enlist employee support for the organization's goals and objectives. In areas such as controlling health care costs, it can foster understanding and support for important company policies.

Editing/Publishing

Closely aligned with internal communications is the editing function. Editing and publishing internal publications was such a key part of the function in the past that the term "editor" was practically a synonym for business communicator. It remains an important function and specialty.

Editing applies to a much wider variety of activities than simply employee publications. Brochures, annual reports, direct mail and marketing pieces, advertising copy, and printed information of all varieties are "edited." As a specialty, "publisher" may be a more apt description, with the communicator responsible for the quality and effectiveness of an organization's printed materials. Sophisticated bulletin board arrangements are also "edited." As new technologies enter the field the editor also may be working with audiovisual communications. Regardless of the medium, the editor serves a management role in supervising the work of others, maintaining cost controls and ensuring efficient production, as well as setting standards of quality in appearance and content.

Electronic Publishing

Recent advances in personal computer hardware and software designed for producing communications documents has created a new specialty—electronic publishing. Software packages specially designed for the purpose enable the communicator to create and shape both graphics and body text on the same screen, and to print original documents on a new breed of "laser" printers.

Creating print pieces in the past has largely consisted of a time-consuming process—having text professionally typeset and then "pasting up" an original. This original would be photographically reproduced as a print plate and copies produced on a printing press. While still in its infancy, electronic publishing offers considerable potential to save a great deal of time and expense in eliminating many of these steps.

Already "newsletters" of surprising quality are appearing from these sources, and at least two new magazines have been founded specifically to serve the electronic publishing industry.

This is a new and growing area which offers opportunities for the innovative to get in on the ground floor, whether as specialists, or simply as communications generalists who would like to have another technological tool in their communications arsenal.

Media Relations

Media relations is the maintenance of a relationship between an organization and the news media—it is hoped a positive one, of mutual benefit to both. This means having individuals trained in the needs and techniques of journalism. It's more than "cranking out" news releases. It means understanding the news gathering process and how your organization fits into that process.

As a staff communicator, the media relations director or specialist may be the organizational spokesman or spokeswoman. In an agency setting the definition of this role may be restricted to matters of "placement," or working with specific media to suggest story ideas, book clients on talk shows, or provide background information on important issues.

The ability to understand and work with the news media is an essential ability of the business communicator as a generalist. It is more likely to be seen as a specialty in an agency environment than within a large organization, although a generalist might find it to be a primary responsibility for a portion of her or his career.

Community Relations

The community relations specialist is concerned with maintaining positive and mutually beneficial relationships between an organization and the many "publics" important to it within the community.

The community relations specialist may represent an organization before community groups, or perhaps coordinate a speakers' bureau which will enable members of the organization to present appropriate messages to important groups. Public relations techniques may apply to community relations, and indeed virtually any communications tool may be called into play if it is deemed the most appropriate for a given message or audience.

Again, the community relations specialist fits the general description of the business communicator—the difference is the audience in which the individual specializes. The communicator advises management on which messages and communications channels should be used to communicate with given "publics" within the community of which the organization is a part.

Public Affairs/Government Relations

Public affairs is closely aligned with community relations, although it typically describes an individual concerned with governmental, regulatory or legislative bodies and activities. The public affairs specialist may be concerned with opinion among various community publics because of their influence on the regulatory process. A business concerned with potential regulation of its manufacturing activities might well be concerned, for instance, with how local residents perceived the company—as an economic boon or environmental albatross. The public affairs specialist would track public sentiment at public hearings, city council meetings, and in the news media. Efforts at the state or federal level to enact regulations would be followed as well.

Public affairs specialists often work closely with legislative advocates (lobbyists) in monitoring and influencing governmental action on issues of interest. In cases where legislative action will effect an organization, for better or worse, the business communicator may call into play public relations techniques to create public awareness and rally public opinion to the organization's cause.

Investor/Financial Relations

Investor relations is a corporate communications specialty, for those businesses which are "publicly held," that is, owned by the public through the sale and purchase of stock. A high value for the business' stock serves the best interests of both the corporation and the investor. The investor relations specialist provides channels of communication to keep shareholders, prospective investors, and security analysts, who make stock recommendations, fully informed.

Other special audiences of the investor/financial relations specialist might be banks or sources of credit for the business. Business and financial writers in the news media may be an important target audience because of their influence and ability to communicate to stockholders and potential investors.

Investor relations specialists also typically supervise the production and dissemination of required financial reports, such as the annual and quarterly reports. They also will ensure that the company complies with regulations of the Security Exchange Commission. Because information about a company can and does affect its stock price, there are legal guidelines as to what kinds of information must be released to the public, as well as the timing and communication channels, which must be used in specific instances.

Complying with these legal requirements and communicating effectively with financial and investment specialists requires considerable expertise both in communications and financial/investment activities.

Opinion Research

Effective opinion research has long been recognized as a vital part of the communication process, both in gaining information necessary for planning and in measuring the results of communication efforts.

Research efforts may be aimed at internal audiences, such as a readership survey concerning an in-house publication, or an evaluation of employee opinion on benefit programs. Research projects may also be targeted at external audiences, such as customers or members of a local community.

This is clearly a specialty area, and only the larger organizations maintain a significant in-house capability for opinion research. There is a sub-industry of research specialists who serve most opinion research needs.

Opinion research is done in a variety of ways, or "methodologies." The written or telephone survey is perhaps the most common, in which a carefully selected series of questions is put to a "sample" of individuals. While asking people their opinions isn't particularly difficult, creating a mechanism to collect information in a way that *accurately* reflects opinion is. It is very easy to introduce bias (inaccuracies) into the questioning process. Selecting a sample of individuals who will reflect a larger public's opinion is a science in itself.

Another technique includes "focus group" meetings, in which a skilled facilitator (meeting leader) participates in a group discussion on issues of interest and evaluates results. Content analysis, or the scientific evaluation of the contents of the news media, is another method.

Opinion research is an area best handled by specialists, and yet the business communications generalist or manager must understand the techniques and principles involved in order to best evaluate and apply the information research produces.

SUMMARY

Ideally, the business communicator in the course of a career will be exposed to most, if not all, of the specialties discussed in this session. The individual considering a career in communications may focus initially on a special area of interest, and delay the decision on whether to diversify and perhaps enter management at a later date. Many of these fields require very different skills and talents to be successful. Others are different only in the target audiences at which they are directed, and a specialist in one might move to another with relative ease.

It would be wise to gain exposure to as many of these fields as possible before making a commitment. Talk to individuals actually working in the field. Visit offices and see what the work actually involves.

For the entry level job seeker, it also may be wise to remain flexible. Focus on what your goals are, to be sure, but be prepared to take opportunities as they present themselves. Even if a position is not precisely what you may want as a long term career, the experience may be generally applicable enough to move you along towards your eventual goal.

Students at the University of Virginia's Colgate Darden Graduate
School of Business Administration explore employment alternatives on
career day. Photo: University of Virginia, Erin Garvey, photographer.

CHAPTER 6

THE JOB SEARCH

FOCUSING ON AN OBJECTIVE

Surprisingly enough, one of the toughest hurdles in an effective job search is narrowing the range of options to a point where the job objective is clear. Newcomers to the job market often fear narrowing their search, presuming that to exclude any options at all lessens their chances of employment. While it's true that remaining flexible is important, particularly for an entry level job seeker, it is far better to focus on what you want, *then* decide to compromise if the situation presents itself. Scattering your resources and efforts across a broad range of possibilities will usually be less effective than focusing precisely on what you desire.

Isn't focusing on business communications enough? It's a good start; but what kind of a business communicator? Do you want to work with an agency? Do you want to be an audiovisual specialist for a major corporation? Or would you prefer to edit a community-oriented magazine for a local hospital?

Different jobs require very different skills, backgrounds, and networking contacts. Employers expect you to tell them exactly what skills you have to offer and what you can do. Saying that you're "willing to give anything a try," may be true, but it isn't going to land you many jobs. If you were the employer, would you prefer that approach to someone who says, "I want to edit an inhouse publication. This is why, and this is what I've done in the past to build the skills necessary to do the job and do it well."

So the beginning of the job search is setting your goals, deciding what you want to do, what you need to do to get there, and how you're going to go about locating job openings and selling yourself to the employer.

MARKETING YOURSELF

Once you've identified your job goal, the next question may be how to market yourself. "Marketing" is a business term for determining what audience will buy or use a product, and how to best inform and persuade that audience to do so. In your case, you want to identify the employers offering the type of positions you're interested in, build the tools that will help you persuade them to hire you, and decide on the approach with the greatest opportunity for success.

FINDING LEADS

A "lead" is a bit of information that will lead you towards an employer offering your job goal. It might be an advertisement in a trade publication, a tip from an acquaintance, or a piece of advice from a professional already working in the field. The more sources of leads you can develop, the better your chances of employment success.

"Networking" is the common term for developing a network of friends, relatives, and professional acquaintances who can provide employment leads. This is easier for the professional who has worked in the field already, but college students can start building their own networks even before they graduate.

Professional organizations offer one ideal form of networking and lead generation. There are numerous professional communications groups which meet regularly and provide professional contacts and other benefits (see Chapter 8). Identifying and participating in these groups is a good first step.

Another technique is the request for informational interviews. In this case you ask for an appointment with professionals in the field, not to interview for a job (although you should be candid that this is your goal), but to ask for opinions and advice. Most people, despite being busy, are willing to help if possible and may be somewhat flattered at being asked for advice. They will be able to provide valuable information, and you may be able to tap into their personal networks to uncover job leads. The best procedure in this case is to write an individual requesting an appointment, then follow up with a phone call. If it is someone you've met at a professional meeting, or if you can say that an acquaintance of the person recommended you contact her or him, so much the better. Informational interviews are also a chance to polish your own interviewing techniques and style prior to getting into the real thing. Treat each one as if it were an honest-to-goodness job interview. Impressions are important. Often these interviews can turn out to be employment producing situations. Make clear in your initial approaches however that you are asking for information, not a job interview, and respect the value of the individual's time.

Informational interviews are different from "cold calls." A cold call is simply a call "out of the blue" asking for a job interview. Or you just walk through the door and ask to see someone about a job. This may occasionally work, but more often it just says "I haven't done my homework to know whether you have a position open or not, but thought I would check anyway." This isn't likely to be as effective as a cover letter saying "I've heard you have such and such a position open, this is why I'm qualified, and I would like to be considered."

WANT ADS

Compared to networking, the want ads of the local newspaper are not particularly fruitful sources of job leads—particularly for entry level jobs. For one thing the competition can be intense. One advertised job opening may literally draw *hundreds* of applicants. Chances are there will always be a few people more qualified than yourself.

Employers dislike the want ad approach as well. They would rather interview someone based on a recommendation from an acquaintance than sift through resumes, which is one reason the networking approach is so effective. It's difficult for an employer to screen a huge number of resumes down to a manageable number for interviews, and the process often becomes arbitrary.

Also, want ads tend to reflect only a small percentage of available jobs. Employment professionals estimate about 80 percent of all openings are never advertised. If you rely on advertisements you'll miss eight out of ten openings.

This isn't to say that you *shouldn't* apply for advertised positions, rather that this should only be a part of your job search efforts. Employment experts suggest you consider the ad carefully, and avoid applying indiscriminately to inappropriate employers or positions you are clearly not qualified for.

They recommend against applying for jobs for which you have only half or fewer of the specified qualifications—chances of getting an interview this way are slim in most situations. If you determine you have two-thirds of the qualifications outlined and can offer skills which can compensate for what you lack, then feel confident in going ahead.

Some job seekers are apprehensive about applying for a position in response to ads from companies they know virtually nothing about. In fact many organizations may run "blind ads," which give only a post office box to respond to.

Career advice columnist Joyce Lain Kennedy suggests studying the wording and quality of the language in help-wanted ads for clues about the type of firm, pay policies, and work environment. She notes, however, that "ultimately— just as the employer checks you out—you'll have to rely on impressions gathered during a job interview and on references from friends and other research resources."

Responding to blind ads is best avoided if possible, particularly if you are currently employed. Individuals have been known to apply to blind ads only to discover it was their own employer looking for someone to replace them!

Beyond local newspapers, there are other "want ad" sources that may be more productive. Trade publications dealing with a particular industry in which you have an interest may carry ads which produce a much smaller response for employers. Professional publications such as *P.R. Journal* (PRSA) or *Communication World* (IABC) carry advertisements for communications positions, although seldom for entry level positions. Regional newsletters (such as *Bulldog* and *BusinessWire* on the West Coast) often carry information on openings.

In addition, IABC maintains "Jobline" which gives information on openings. PRSA has a job service, and local chapters of most professional associations maintain a job listing service either in their offices or in a regular publication.

LIBRARIES AS RESOURCES

University libraries are an excellent resource, especially for examining specialized publications for job leads.

Libraries also carry numerous directories of professional organizations, employers in certain industries and fields, associations, advertising and public relations agencies, and other useful information. This is the place to invest your time prior to sending out so-called "broadcast" cover letters and resumes, which are the job seekers version of a mass-mailing. See Appendix (A), Directory bibliography.

JOB LINES

Job lines are another little-used source of job leads. Both the International Association of Business Communicators and the Public Relations Society of America maintain phone lines which may be dialed for recorded information on current openings. Here too, entry-level openings are an exception. Similarly, many local professional organizations operate "job banks", where openings are publicized, usually at monthly meetings, and resumes are retained on file for employers to review.

HEADHUNTERS

Executive recruiters, or "headhunters", are a job lead source which is usually restricted to experienced professionals. These search firms seek senior individuals who qualify for high-paying, high responsibility jobs. They are useful if you fit into that category, but will seldom be cooperative unless you can command a hefty salary in whatever position they might place you. See Appendix (B) for a listing of search firms specializing in communications.

THE NUMBERS GAME

The more lead sources you can develop the sooner you will be able to find the job you want. The tried and true network approach is still the best. College students can start off with their professors, many of whom maintain contacts with previous graduates. As you progress through your career you will find it advantageous to maintain your own professional contacts and personal network, so that in the event you find yourself in need of a new and better job you will have friends to call upon. Keep that in mind if you find yourself in a position to do someone else a favor along the way. Good deeds have a way of returning.

THE TOOLS: THE RESUME, COVER LETTER, WRITING ADDENDUM, PORTFOLIO, INTERVIEW

Resumes

Once you've identified your employment objective, there are a variety of tools which will be useful in marketing yourself.

The most common of these is the resume. The resume is a simple one or two page statement of your background, experience, accomplishments and employment objectives. It should be clear, concise and to the point. The purpose of the resume is not so much to get a job as to get a job interview. Used in conjunction with a cover letter, it is a primary job search tool.

There are numerous books offering detailed advice on

preparing a resume, and these should be consulted, particularly if you're putting one together for the first time. There are, however, several points which need to be made about a prospective business communicator's resume.

For one thing, you will be applying for a communications job. This means the employer will look at the resume as an example of your ability to communicate. It must be perfect in all respects. Is the lay-out precise and easily read? Is the typing professional? Does the content show an ability to combine an organized, structured approach with writing which is clear and to the point?

Above all the resume must be free of errors. All too often the employer is dealing with many resumes, and may be looking for an excuse to screen some out. Mistakes—even simple typing errors—provide that excuse. Misspellings virtually guarantee rejection.

The resume will be the example of your ability to communicate. It will represent you during the crucial first contact. The time spent to polish it and make it perfect is time well spent.

If you've focused your job search sufficiently, you should be able to tailor your resume to each potential job appropriately. Type each resume individually. Consider the needs of the employer and the demands of the job; and write each resume accordingly. Don't have your resume professionally typeset and printed. While it may look nice, it says to the employer: "I'm unemployed and sending this standard resume to everyone I can think of." The tailored, typewritten resume says, "I'm especially interested in *your* opening."

A resume is not just a list of prior experience. If experience is your strong point, sure, play it up. If not, focus on your education, involvement in community or professional groups, freelance writing, awards, or whatever other strengths you may have.

How do Employers Evaluate Resumes?

According to a poll of personnel managers conducted by Northwest University, experience remains the single most important part of a resume. For an inexperienced entry-level job however, managers say a high grade point average is "very important."

When asked, "what are the most important items you consider when evaluating a resume?", 30 percent of the personnel managers surveyed said work experience. Twenty-four percent said academic background, and 13 percent said grades. Career objectives, and clarity and neatness, were each noted by 10 percent.

Asked how much importance the company attaches to a high grade point when evaluating an inexperienced entry level candidate, 68 percent said "important" or "very important," 17 percent were ambivalent, and 15 percent said grade point was "not very important."

For examples of an entry level resume and an advanced communicator's resume see Appendices C and D.

The Cover Letter

In most cases your resume will be accompanied by a cover letter. Again, in the communications field this will be a sample of your writing and communicating ability. And remember, writing ability is one of the most important talents of a business communicator. Use your cover letter to showcase your ability to write in a clear, comprehensible fashion. That doesn't mean being tricky or cute, it means laying out your background, qualifications and suitability for the position in an efficient, readable style. Be brief, concise, don't waste the employer's valuable time. Make your points, but stick to one page. You don't need to repeat your resume, it will be there as an enclosure, but highlight those aspects of your background which specifically apply to the position in question.

Keep in mind that the purpose of sending a cover letter and resume is to get an interview. Your goal is to interest the employer sufficiently in your abilities to warrant a further investment of time. Your resume and cover letter are not the place for communicating everything about yourself in exhaustive detail. Keep the purpose in mind as you prepare it. Be brief, sell yourself without being boastful, and don't be embarrassed about asking for a job—employers need good people just as much as you need a good employer, often more. (See sample cover letter Appendix F)

Writing Addendum

A tool of considerable value to the communications professional is the writing addendum, or bibliography of your writing and project accomplishments. This is an important adjunct to your resume for a variety of reasons. For one, writing is an absolute prerequisite for most communications jobs. You must establish yourself as a competent writer, and the writing addendum does this. The resume, being concise, does not allow for elaboration on writing and communication accomplishments, the writing addendum does.

Oddly, the writing addendum is not widely used. The individual with the foresight to put one together has an advantage over the competition. The mere presence of a writing addendum demonstrates initiative, organization and planning ability—all valuable qualities to the employer.

The addendum can also help shape an interview, guiding the interviewer through your accomplishments. It complements your portfolio, offering a listing of projects which might be too extensive to actually show physically. It can demonstrate your breadth of experience and capabilities.

The writing addendum should essentially be a bibliography of your writing efforts—*all* of those you consider reasonably significant. They don't have to be published, by-lined, or even entirely your own work (as long as you acknowledge that). Subheadings might highlight the various areas in which you've written, such as published work, copywriting, technical writing, position papers, speeches, broadcast scripting, and on. It may be tailored to your particular writing accomplishments or to the needs of the employer.

The addendum should note that "samples are available upon request," although strictly speaking you aren't obligated to be able to physically produce every piece of writing mentioned.

If you are asked to furnish samples, take advantage of the opportunity by also providing information on how the writing was successful or contributed to the accomplishment of an organization's objectives. You can do this by attaching a card with the salient facts.

A writing addendum can be started at any time, even before a student graduates from school or a potential lateral move candidate has actually worked in the field. Sources of work can include classwork, the school newspaper, press releases for volunteer organizations, internships, and freelance writing of all varieties.

The writing addendum, like the portfolio, is a tool which should be continually added to and updated throughout the professional communicator's career. The more experience you gain and accomplishments you achieve, the better they will be. Keep in mind, however, that even for the beginner merely having a well-prepared writing addendum sets you apart from the competition as one of those with a little extra going for them. See Appendix E for a sample writing addendum.

Portfolio

Another job search tool is the portfolio. This is distinct from the first three in that it is for use during the interview process. A portfolio is a carefully prepared selection of previous work, including writing, photography, design, and editing and may include brochures, advertisements, published articles—whatever work samples best represent your talents and coincide with the needs of the employer. The portfolio is composed of concrete examples of work which demonstrate your ability to accomplish the tasks required in the new position.

Art and business supply stores carry various types of portfolio binders with protective plastic sleeves. Make it a habit to keep samples of everything you do, and continue to maintain and upgrade your portfolio as your career progresses. It is never too soon to begin one, and never too late to improve it. As with the writing addendum, a well-prepared portfolio can give you an edge in a tough competition.

In addition to work samples, the portfolio may include copies of your resume and writing addendum, educational transcripts, letters of reference, and names and addresses of references. The portfolio can be one of your most effective sales tools, and it too should be tailored to the specific position and employer which has been targeted.

Remember what your portfolio is supposed to achieve. It should be designed to create a favorable impression. Appearance and organization are just as important as content. A manila folder of tattered writing samples is going to hurt you—even if the writing is great. An interviewer will seldom take the time to seriously read *all* the materials in a portfolio, mainly because there's limited time, and you're there to be *interviewed,* not sit and watch the personnel director read writing samples.

The portfolio should be an attractive package that the interviewer can rapidly flip through and get an idea of the type of work you've done. It should have a insert pocket in the back in which you should keep copies of writing samples *to leave behind,* so the interviewer can review them at her or his convenience.

If the interviewer would like to keep the portfolio for more detailed examination after the interview, so much the better. Returning to pick it up at a later date will give you a chance to follow up on the interview. The interviewer may also want to show the portfolio to others involved in the decision-making process to justify a choice or to solicit opinions. In either case a topnotch portfolio is very much in your favor.

Interviews

The hoped-for outcome of sending your resume, cover letter, and writing addendum to an employer is an invitation to participate in an interview. The interview is your opportunity to learn more about the position, discuss fully your own experience and qualifications for the job, and to display your work in the form of the portfolio.

Again, there are numerous books which explore in detail the techniques of conducting a successful interview. And, as with the resume, the interview will be a special gauge of your effectiveness as a communicator. An engineer might be forgiven for a reticent manner and stumbling speech, an applicant for a position as company spokesperson probably would not. Communicators are expected to remain poised and articulate under pressure. They may represent their organizations to the news media and outside groups, often under stress. Their appearance and manner is vitally important. They must be able to express themselves well, on a one-to-one basis just as much as in writing. The interview will be a test of the applicant's ability to do this. If you find interviews abnormally difficult (they aren't easy for anybody), you will probably want to practice on friends or relatives until you are comfortable with your abilities.

Go into an interview prepared. Know the company, the position, and how you can fit in and contribute to the organization. Impressions are extremely important. An employer wants people who are punctual (never be late for a job interview), who are poised, articulate, intelligent and personable. In the interview process you'll be sized up as much for the type of person you are as for your capabilities. The employer will want to know not only if you can do the job, but if you will fit in and work well with others in the organization.

After the interview is completed several things still remain for you to do. Send a letter thanking the individual for the interview and confirming any important points of the discussion. If you promised to send anything, such as work samples or references, be sure to do so promptly. If you promised to check back by phone or personally visit then do so, *when* you said you would. If you were given other names to contact, then follow up.

SUMMARY

Your job search should be approached as a marketing problem. Research and explore the communications opportunities in your area of interest. Find out who the employers are and what their needs are. Prepare a strategy for developing leads which will enable you to contact these organizations as openings occur. Develop your sales tools—the resume, cover letter, writing addendum and portfolio. Practice your personal interviewing and communication style.

The job search is a planned, coordinated effort which ties together. Depending upon your talents, experience and job goals, it may be an easy search or a difficult one. If you are firm in your goals, and either have the talents or are willing to develop them, a determined and systematic job search will pay off for you. Communications is a growing field and the need is there. Be confident, and remember that the more prepared you are, the easier it will be.

The ability to work with facts and figures by computer is a great asset for a corporate business communicator. Photo: First National Bank of Chicago.

CHAPTER 7

THE CAREER PATH

When a man does not know what harbor he is making for, no wind is the right wind.

Lucius Seneca
Roman Philosopher

All too often the main consideration in an individual career decision is, "What will I be doing next month, or six months from now?"

According to Len Daniels, President of Placement Associates, Inc., which specializes in communications positions, "People who make logical and well thought out career moves generally fare better economically and emotionally in the long run and enjoy a higher degree of professional respect than the indiscriminate job-hopper."

Choosing a career, or making a career change, is one of the most important decisions you can make, with repercussions involving where and how you live, how you spend your working hours, and what your future prospects will be.

A "career" as opposed to a "job," is the continuing flow of events which takes an individual from entry-level-job A to ultimate-goal-objective Z. The career path is a combination of experience, education, training, and professional contacts which combine to provide both the qualifications and the opportunities to achieve the long-term career goals which have been set. It may or may not be entirely with a single organization. Increasingly it means changing organizations several times during a career, perhaps returning to school for an advanced degree, or varying levels of participation in professional groups.

The most important single step is viewing your current position, or job goal, as part of your career—a part of that continuing process of moving upward. A systematic approach is invaluable. Set both short and long term goals. Keep those goals before you, continually reminding you to be alert for opportunities to move closer to achieving them.

Focus on your goals—what you want to achieve. Develop a plan—what has to be done to achieve goals, what qualifications are needed? Then implement the plan—do it, adjust it if necessary; but stick with it and *do it*!

THE QUESTIONS

As you consider a career in communications, there are several questions which must be faced. First of all, how far, and how fast, do you want to go? Remember that it is important to set reasonable goals in order to avoid frustration. Yet at the same time you should set goals which require you to stretch, to perform to the best of your ability, to achieve what you're capable of.

Where do you want to be in 10 years, in 20? Is your long-term goal to be in communication management, or to be a specialist? The career paths to these are very different. Do you want broad-based experience in a wide variety of communication techniques, or do you want the maximum possible skill and experience in a single communication specialty—such as speech writing or audiovisual production.

What is important to you? Is it money? Responsibility?

Geographic location? Future opportunities? Job satisfaction? Or, more likely, a individualized combination of all of these?

How important to you is security? Will you feel more comfortable with a single, probably large, organization which might offer long-term career opportunities? Or are you willing to trade security for the greater responsibilities and potential for rapid advancement which a small firm might offer?

No one can answer these questions for you. You will have to answer them for yourself. Frankly, this isn't always easy. Sometimes we discover that the reality of a certain job or organization is different from what we expected, or we didn't enjoy it in the way we anticipated. Flexibility is a necessity as times, people, and organizations constantly change.

What is certain, though, and vitally important is to adopt a "career-minded" approach to your employment, to focus on defined goals, and to continue to move towards those goals.

IABC CAREER MATRIX SKILL LEVELS

As an aid to its members, the International Association of Business Communicators publishes a "career matrix" designed to identify the various career progression levels of a professional business communicator, and the skills typically found at those levels. This information is particularly helpful in planning out a "career plan" which will provide the experience and skills necessary to move steadily up the career ladder.

The IABC matrix defines seven career levels.

Level I is the beginning professional (assumed to have a degree in journalism, organizational communication, or a related field).

Level II is the staff professional. This might be a communications specialist in a corporate setting, an account assistant in an agency environment, or perhaps a junior grade public affairs officer in the military.

Level III is the professional manager—an agency account executive, a GS 11-13 in government, or a corporate communications manager.

Level IV is the professional director, including account supervisors with agencies, a major to lieutenant colonel in the military, or a GS 12-14 in government.

Level V is an organizational officer or seasoned professional director. This would include agency vice presidents, full colonel public affairs officers, and GS 15 government workers.

Level VI is the senior communications officer or senior professional director level. This would include corporate vice presidents of public relations, senior officers of public relations agencies, and senior public affairs military personnel (below the rank of general/admiral).

Level VII, the highest level, represents the most senior communications positions available, including chief executive officers of public relations agencies, senior vice presidents of corporate communications, senior consultants, senior executives in government agencies, and general/admiral rank officers in the armed forces.

Skills to Match the IABC Levels

The skills listed below are those normally expected of an individual at the level indicated. There is some overlap, and individuals at the higher levels are assumed to have the experience and skills of the lower levels.

This matrix provides a valuable tool in setting career goals, identifying skills and experience necessary to advance, and developing a strategy to obtain those skills and experience.

Level	
I, II	Communication theory
I, II	Writing news
I, II	Writing features
I, II	Newsletter editing and layout
I, II	Magazine editing and layout
I, II	Photography basics
I, II, III	Graphic design
I, II, III	Writing for A/V and video
I, II, III	Law and government relations
I, II, III	Speakers' bureaus
I, II, III, IV	Event and conference planning and support
I, II, III, IV	Speech writing
All levels	Communication ethics
II, III	Writing proposals
II, III	Slide/tape and AV production
II, III	Video production
II, III	Film production
II, III	Print production
II, III	Publications management
II, III	Use of electronic distribution systems
II, III	Basic data processing applications
II, III	General management skills
II, III, IV	Media contact
II, III, IV	Budgeting and cost control
II, III, IV	Personnel supervision
II, III, IV	Audience/constituent research
II, III, IV	Feedback systems

II, III, IV, V	Writing the communication action plan
III, IV	Investor/shareholder relations
III, IV	Writing policies and procedures
III, IV	Identity programs
III, IV	Time management
III, IV	Member communication
III, IV	Personnel interviewing/selection
III, IV	Goal setting
III, IV	Measurement of effectiveness
III, IV, V	Computers in communication management
III, IV, V	Communication in support of marketing
III, IV, V	Employee communication program management
III, IV, V	Organizational culture and politics
III, IV, V, VI	Community relations program management
III, IV, V, VI, VII	Project management
III, IV, V, VI, VII	Public speaking techniques
III, IV, V, VI, VII	Consulting skills/problem solving
IV, V	Financial communication programs
IV, V	Managing communication staff
IV, V	Crisis communication management
IV, V, VI	Media relations management
IV, V, VI	Labor relations communication management
IV, V, VI	Marketing communication function to senior management
IV, V, VI	Managing corporate contributions
IV, V, VI	Accountability management
IV, V, VI, VII	Group/meetings management

IV, V, VI, VII	Issues management
IV, V, VI, VII	Strategic communications planning
IV, V, VI, VII	Communication policy formation
V, VI, VII	Organizational design
V, VI, VII	International communication management
V, VI, VII	Government affairs/legislation
V, VI, VII	Political Action Committee design and management
V, VI, VII	Labor relations
V, VI, VII	Marketing
V, VI, VII	Financial management
V, VI, VII	Problem analysis/identification
V, VI, VII	Research

PERSONAL EVALUATION AND CAREER PLANNING

To get an idea of how the career matrix information might apply to you, use the following exercise developed by the IABC for its members to evaluate their current job status and to assist in focusing on future career goals:

Exercise

Get a pencil and paper. Ready?

As quickly as you can, list three terms that could have been applied to describe you five years ago.

Under that list, write *Today* and then quickly list three things which you are today.

Now write a 5 and list three things you wish to be in five years.

Repeat the process for three things you wish to be in *10* years.

If you wish, make a list for *15* years.

Now look at the lists. Most people will have at least one work-related item in each list. Yesterday's list may say, "student," today's "editor," and the 10 or 15-year list may include "vice president for public relations."

Most of us tend to list work-related functions because work is a large part of our lives. This is especially true of communicators because they usually see their work as being something more than a job.

If you don't have work-related items on your lists, you may wish to take a close look at yourself and your career plans to determine if you are in, or are considering, the right profession.

Now look closely at the work-related items on your lists. Have you advanced over the last five years? Why? Why not? If the answer is "yes," evaluate what helped you accomplish that advancement and write down those things. If the answer is "no," is it because you lack some skills, because times have been tough in your organization, or because you are content to stay right where you are?

Look at your lists for the next 5, 10, and 15 years. Do you want to advance? How are you going to do it? Will the techniques you used in the past work in the future?

Let's assume for a moment that you're an average communicator and you've been with your organization long enough to have an idea of how some of those ahead of you have gotten where they are. That may be helpful to know, but remember that the field is changing so rapidly, and the tools used are changing so fast, that what worked in the past may not be what's needed in the future.

Further, will your current organization offer you the opportunity to be where you want to be in 5, 10, or 15 years? Do you *want* to stay with it?

If you do want to stay with your current organization, how do you make yourself so visible and valuable that they've just *got* to keep you and may decide to move you along?

What skills on your list of needs do you wish to acquire? What skills do you wish to avoid? If you wish to avoid some skills needed for advancement to higher levels, will you have other skills strong enough to make up for that lack? Finally, what are you good at, and who is willing to pay you to do it?

Write down the answers to these questions. These answers will help prepare you for the next step, mapping out your career or professional development plan.

Drafting a Career Plan

To put your career goals in writing, use the following technique in conjunction with the IABC career matrix:

Take a piece of paper and label it "Personal Career Plan—Fifteen Years." List columns across the top of the paper, starting with "position goal." Then list column headings of "skills required," "level," "where to obtain," "time span," and "costs."

- Establish 5-10-15-year goals.
- List a goal you want to achieve by the end of that time.
- List the skills required to achieve that goal both from the matrix and any other special requirements for your company or industry.
- Note the skills you already have and consider those you may need.
- Determine ways to obtain the skills you have not mastered. List several possible ways. Keep in mind that in addition to obtaining the skills, you may have to prove to an employer that you have the skills. Therefore, in addition to attending a seminar, you may also want to demonstrate your skill through some sort of practice.

- Determine where and when opportunities are available and the costs associated with those opportunities.
- Set up a plan based on available time. Include *start* and *complete* dates.

Remember, don't try to take on too much in terms of either time or cost. Be realistic.

Keep your plan in a file and review it periodically, noting progress. Adapt and change it to accommodate new opportunities, ideas, and thoughts on personal career direction as they occur to you. Personal career planning should be an ongoing, continuous activity.*

TIPS FOR MOVING AHEAD

As you can tell from the previous sections, organizations such as the IABC devote considerable attention to the professional development and career advancement of their members. Membership in such professional groups can be of considerable assistance throughout a career (see Chapter 8).

Another reason for careful career planning is that it helps avoid the common tendency to evaluate a job strictly on the basis of salary. If you know what you want to do, where you want to go, and what you have to do to get there, it will be easier to say no to a job opportunity which might pay more in the short run but would throw you off your planned career path. Abandoning a carefully laid plan in favor of short term monetary gain may delay your move upward and hurt you monetarily in the long run.

---

*Planning exercise reprinted courtesy of the International Association of Business Communicators.

Developing a "network" of professional contacts as you move through your chosen career path is another key part of upward career mobility. This is particularly important if your career path involves moving from one organization to another. Professional contacts are essential in finding out when employment opportunities are available, and in providing support during awkward periods of transition from one organization to another.

Probably the single most important ingredient of career success is pursuing a career which you enjoy. You won't necessarily enjoy every day and every second of it, but most of the time you should enjoy what you do. If you don't enjoy your job, you probably won't do your very best work, which means you won't advance as rapidly as those around you.

SUMMARY

A job decision often revolves around what's best for today, for here and now. A career decision involves much more, including the effect of today's job decision on your chances of reaching a career goal 5 years, 10 years, or 15 years down the road.

Focusing on your career goals and developing a plan to acquire the skills and experience necessary to achieve them is one of the most important steps towards your eventual success as a professional business communicator.

Career planning, and movement up the career ladder, is an intentional activity that should be a continuous part of your professional experience.

While much of what has been covered in this chapter might apply to any career field, the need to be systematic, flexible, and organized in business communication will be particularly great in the decades ahead. The field is constantly changing, the tools and techniques, the types of experience necessary, and the way in which the job is done is subject to constant revision.

Given this constant state of change, new career opportunities, as they open up, will go to those who have best anticipated and prepared for them. Business communications will be a challenging, rewarding career for those willing to learn and adapt themselves. For those who are content to occupy a certain niche within an organization, doing a certain task in the same way again and again, a communications career will be hazardous indeed, for the field will probably pass them by.

Excitement, innovation and challenge will be the hallmark of the communications career on into the next century. For the right person, with the right objectives and attitude toward planned career growth, it will be a rewarding experience.

CHAPTER 8

PROFESSIONAL ORGANIZATIONS

BUSINESS COMMUNICATIONS ORGANIZATIONS

Most professions are served by professional organizations—groups of individuals with common interests and career objectives. Business communications is no exception. Two of the most prominent communications-oriented groups are the International Association of Business Communicators (IABC), and the Public Relations Society of America (PRSA). Both have chapters in nearly every part of America and IABC in many other countries as well.

Professional groups serve many purposes. They provide a means for communicators to meet, interact, and network. They support the work and professional development of members through seminars, conferences, workshops and publication of books and professional journals. They are composed of and operated by professional communicators for the benefit of the profession and its members.

WHO ARE THE MEMBERS?

Some organizations require prospective members to be actively working in the field, others offer affiliate memberships for those with an interest in communications.

Virtually all organizations have special provisions for student members, or sponsor nearby student chapters.

Demographic descriptions of the members of both the IABC and PRSA are provided in sections dealing with those groups.

ASSISTING THE JOB SEARCH

For the job seeker, professional organizations can greatly assist networking efforts by placing the candidate in the mainstream of the professional community. Even if the job seeker doesn't actually join each organization, just attending monthly luncheon meetings and participating in special events provide opportunities to meet people and gain information.

There can be a surprising selection of professional communications groups in a single community, including chapters of national organizations and strictly local entities. In Sacramento, California, for example, communications groups include the IABC, the Sacramento Public Relations Round Table, State Public Information Officers Council, Association for Multi-Image, Association of Sacramento Advertising Photographers, Sacramento Women in Advertising, Ad Club, Art Directors and Artists Club, Sacramento Valley Marketing Association, Sacramento Area Technical Communicators Association, and Women in Communications.

A typical monthly meeting will consist of a luncheon or dinner where business is taken care of and members hear a guest speaker. These monthly gatherings are an excellent opportunity to meet and talk with professional communicators, many of whom will be able to assist in a job search. Many groups maintain "job banks" where openings are listed, or resumes are kept on file for employers to review.

Openings are often announced by members during meetings as well.

The IABC maintains a "job line" phone service in San Francisco and Toronto. PRSA provides one in New York City. These services can be called for recorded information on current job openings. However, these openings are rarely for entry level positions.

Many organizations have student chapters, which offer a chance to begin the networking process even while still in school. A recent graduate can reaffiliate as a regular member with a chapter in the desired geographical area of employment, and will find membership provides an "introduction" to the professional communications community which might otherwise take much more time to obtain.

To take full advantage of professional groups members should be active in various committees—such as scholarship, professional development, community service, etc. Actually working with people on a project is the best way to get to know them, and to give them an opportunity to get to know you. Newcomers are welcome, regardless of experience level, because assistance in volunteer organizations is always needed.

Another advantage of membership is that participation in professional groups (listed on resumes) demonstrates commitment to the profession and sends the right signals to potential employers.

AIDING CAREER DEVELOPMENT

The creation of a network of professional contacts who can assist you throughout your career is an ongoing process. Professional contacts can help you should you find yourself in need of new employment, can steer you towards career opportunities you might otherwise be unaware of, and can provide a support system to strengthen your job performance and movement towards career objectives. Membership in professional groups is the best single way of building such relationships.

Professional groups also offer guidance and assistance in developing the skills necessary to advance in the field. The IABC, for example, publishes a "professional development guide" complete with a career matrix which defines levels of professional growth and the skills necessary to achieve them. (Abbreviated in Chapter 7).

INTERNATIONAL ASSOCIATION OF BUSINESS COMMUNICATORS

The International Association of Business Communicators (IABC) is headquartered at 870 Market Street, Suite 940, San Francisco, California 94102, (415) 433-3400. The organization has more than 12,000 members, with 123 chapters throughout the United States, Canada, the United Kingdom, Hong Kong, and the Philippines.

The IABC's mission statement is:

> IABC is dedicated to the improvement of organizational communication. To this end, the association will seek to enhance the professional competence of those engaged in communications and will provide them with comprehensive tools, techniques and resources.
>
> IABC fully recognizes that communication is undergoing vast and rapid change. Thus, the association will serve to make the managements of organizations fully

aware of the value of effective communications and the role of professional communicators in helping to meet organizational objectives.

Demographics of IABC Membership

Median Age: 34. Male/Female Ratio: 40/60
Major field of study: Journalism
Median Salary: $29,000

49.0%	Corporate
12.5%	Not-For-Profit
8.4%	Financial Institution
5.8%	Hospital/Medical
5.1%	Educational Institution
4.5%	Counseling Firms
4.5%	Government
6.0%	Self-Employed

24.3%	Communications
17.4%	Public Relations
8.2%	Public Affairs
8.2%	Personnel
7.6%	Marketing/Advertising
5.6%	Public Information
3.9%	Internal Communications
3.4%	Community Relations
2.8%	Corporate Relations
2.4%	Administration

Dues

International dues are presently $110 per year but are always subject to change. Chapter dues vary by location. There is a one-time $25 new member application fee.

Services:

The IABC "Jobline" job bank service, (415) 421-9342, provides up-to-date, recorded information on job openings.

The "Communication Bank" provides a skills network and clearinghouse of resources gathered from more than 1,500 international resources. For a nominal fee, booklets of information on a wide variety of communication topics are available, as well as a collection of actual materials available on a loan basis.

The IABC holds numerous district conferences, usually in the fall, and an annual international conference. Professional development seminars are featured at these and other events.

Publication

A monthly four-color publication, *Communication World,* is described as "a magazine reporting on new ideas, people, issues and other information designed to keep communications and public relations professionals informed of what is happening in the industry."

Award Program

An annual "Gold Quill Awards" contest is sponsored, with 85 categories to enter, including communication programs and campaigns; special communication projects; audiovisuals; annual reports; magazines; newspapers & magapapers; newsletters; special publications; design; writing; and photography.

Student Chapters

Approximately 56 student chapters totaling 2,000 members exist at educational institutions, and student membership in regular chapters is permitted. Student dues: $25.

PUBLIC RELATIONS SOCIETY OF AMERICA

The Public Relations Society of America (PRSA) is headquartered at 845 Third Avenue, New York, NY 10022, (212) 826-1750. The PRSA has 91 chapters throughout the United States.

Mission Statement

To serve the public need for understanding and cooperation among its diverse interests by fostering high professional and ethical standards for all those practicing public relations.

Demographics

Median Age: 41. Male/Female Ratio: 60/40
Major field of study: Journalism
Median Salary: $35,000

35%	Corporate
31%	Counseling Firms
12%	Not-For Profit
7%	Education
6%	Healthcare
5%	Government/Military

5%	Utilities
5%	Freelance Consultants

20%	Senior Managers
27%	Managers in Counseling Firms
31%	Middle Managers for Public Relations Programs
24%	Media Relations
22%	Researchers, Writers
13%	Publications

Dues

Dues are presently $150 per year, with an application fee of $50.

Services

The PRSA "Professional Connection" job bank service (212) 308-7284, provides recorded information on current job openings.

The PRSA Information Center contains the world's largest library of public relations texts, articles, guidebooks, etc., and services approximately 20,000 requests each year.

Chapters, districts and PRSA sections hold seminars, with the Forum Series sponsored by the national organization. Conferences are held at numerous levels throughout the year.

Publication

Public Relations Journal, a monthly magazine, is "edited for public relations practitioners and educators." Its editorial scope is "to alert public relations men and women to social, political and economic issues, as well as new developments, ideas and techniques in the public relations field, to present articles dealing with management and communications problems as well as successful solutions to such problems."

Award Program

The PRSA's "Silver Anvil" awards constitute a major international public relations competition of significant prestige. There are 38 categories to enter in this competition, including community relations; institutional programs; special events and observances; public service; marketing communication; international public relations; emergency public relations; internal communications and special public relations programs.

Student Chapters

The Public Relations Student Society of America in 1985 had 4,218 members, and 137 chapters. Annual membership dues are $25.

OTHER PROFESSIONAL ORGANIZATIONS

American Society of Hospital Marketing and Public Relations
840 North Lake Shore Drive
Chicago, IL 60611
(312) 280-6359

Formerly the American Society of Hospital Public Relations. Membership is $75-120 per year. Publishes

"Hospital Marketing and Public Relations" bimonthly.

Association for Business Communication
English Building
608 S. Wright St.
Urbana, IL 61801
(217) 333-1007

Membership consists of teachers, training directors, business executives and consultants. Membership: $30 per year.

Association for Multi-Image International
8019 N. Himes Ave. Suite 401
Tampa, FL 33614
(813) 932-1692

Members are actively engaged in the field of multi-image production use. Promotes the use of multi-image as a medium for education, communication and entertainment. Membership: $75 per year.

Council of Communication Societies
Box 1074
Silver Spring, MD 20910
(301) 953-5000

A federation of autonomous associations working to improve human communications through language and the graphic arts.

Health Sciences Communications Association
Route 5, Box 311F
Midlothian, VA 23113
(804) 794-0363

A professional association of individuals interested in application of educational technology to the health sciences field. Membership: $65 per year.

Industrial Communication Council
Box 3970, Grand Central Station
New York, NY 10163
(212) 254-3985

Individuals in member companies responsible for communication with the public, government and employees. Membership $125 per year. Publishes the ICC newsletter monthly.

International Communication Association
Suite 828, 12750 Merit Drive
Dallas, TX 75251
(214) 233-3889

Founded in 1948 originally as the National Society for the Study of Communication, this organization encourages the systematic study of communication theories, processes and skills.

International Labor Communications Association
815 16th St., N.W.
Room 509
Washington, DC 20006
(202) 347-5564

Members are editors of union publications.

Issues Management Association
1090 Vermont Ave., N.W., Suite 928
Washington, DC 20005
(202) 682-1548

Members are corporate/government executives and academics concerned with the effect of public issues on corporate policy. Membership: $75 a year. Publishes "Issues Managers' Newsletter" monthly.

National Association of County Information Officers
440 First St., N.W.
Washington, DC 20001
(202) 393-6226

Members are county public information officers and staff.

National Investor Relations Institute
1730 M St., N.W., Suite 806
Washington, DC 20036
(202) 861-0630

A professional association of corporate officers and investor relations consultants. Membership $250 a year.

National School Public Relations Association
1801 N. Moore St.
Arlington, VA 22209
(703) 528-5840

Individuals from school districts, national, state and local associations, state education agencies, school-community relations programs, and information agencies.

Railroad Public Relations Association
405 American Railroads Bldg.
Washington, DC 30036
(202) 835-9561

Members include railroad public relations officers, public relations officers from allied industries and editors of railroad industry publications. Membership $50 per year.

Religious Public Relations Council
The Interchurch Center
Room 1031, 475 Riverside Drive
New York, NY 10115
(212) 870-2013

Open to individuals devoting a major portion of their service in professional public relations to any religious community, organization, or related agency. Membership $60 per year.

Women in Communications
Box 9561
Austin, Texas 78766
(512) 346-9875

With 208 chapters across the United States, this organization seeks to improve women's opportunities in the communications professions.

SUMMARY

If you are considering a career in business communications, there is no better way to meet and talk with people who are currently working in the field than through professional organizations. Such contact can help provide a realistic view of the profession, thereby avoiding future disappointments. Nothing is worse than spending four years in college preparing for a profession and discovering it isn't anything like what you had anticipated.

Once in the career field, professional organizations offer a wide variety of career enhancing benefits. More than anything, they offer a chance to meet and interact with other professionals. This interaction, enriching in and of itself, is also an excellent avenue to build contacts and "networks" within the profession which will enhance and assist the individual's career as a business communicator.

CHAPTER 9

FREELANCING

Of all human lots for a person of sensibility that of an
obscure free lance in literature or journalism is, I think,
the most discouraging. It was during this period that I
wrote The Red Badge of Courage.

Stephen Crane

The term freelance dates back to the days of the mounted
knight, when the allegiance for hire of an unattached knight
was referred to as a "free lance."

In today's terminology the term usually describes a writer
whose services are available for hire, but may also describe a
photographer, audiovisual specialist, graphic designer, or
other communications professional. *Freelancers* do not
work as employees, but rather offer their services as needed,
usually on a project basis. When services are offered in evaluating, planning and implementing communication efforts,
the term *consultant* is more likely to be used.

EDITORIAL, MARKETING, AND
TECHNICAL COMMUNICATIONS

Ernest Mau in *The Free-Lance Writer's Survival Guide*
breaks freelance activity into three categories: editorial,
marketing, and technical.

Editorial communications is associated with the news media or publishing industry. The "glamour" field of writing, this includes the writing of books, magazine articles, and other materials where the author receives a byline, or credit, for her or his work, and varying levels of public attention. Many freelancers are attracted to this area by the lure of seeing their work in print, but it is a very competitive area. With the exception of a relatively few, highly-talented individuals beginning writers are unlikely to make a living of it as a full-time job. There are, however, many positive aspects of writing editorial communications, which will be examined shortly.

Marketing communications deals with the realms of public relations, advertising, and sales. Rather than providing a "story" to the news media, magazine, or entertainment field, the freelancer in marketing is more likely to be working with a business organization producing materials designed to be persuasive. These might be advertisements, new product news releases, sales brochures, or perhaps the script for a public service announcement. Businesses often turn to outside help when in need of special expertise or when current workloads are too much for inhouse staff.

Technical communications has recently been a growing area of freelance activity, usually involving technical writing for marketing and non-marketing support of a business' products. This area includes technical manuals, procedures, and engineering documents, and is a type of writing which requires specialized technical knowledge. Opportunities in this area promise to expand as new technologies continue to appear in engineering, computer fields, medicine, and other high-tech fields.

These three categories—editorial, marketing, and technical communications—encompass much of the freelance market. They are areas which all business communicators can expect to encounter and be called upon to be competent in, whether as a regular employee or on a freelance basis.

WHY FREELANCE?

Clearly, many communicators are attracted to freelance writing because if offers a much greater degree of freedom than work as a regular employee. The freelancer sets her or his own hours, controls the type of projects to be worked on, and within limits when, where, and how they work.

The other side of the coin is that a freelancer is a self-employed business person, without the security of a regular paycheck, employee benefits, and the dependability of a regular job.

Many business communicators will find their involvement in freelancing to be less than full-time employment. The nature of freelancing is such that it lends itself to work as time and resources permit. A communicator who works for a business primarily in a marketing capacity may write editorial materials for the enjoyment of it. A technical writer may do marketing materials to polish skills and improve opportunities for future advancement.

A common phenomenon is for a business communicator to enter the ranks of management and find that on-the-job writing opportunities have diminished, as planning and supervisory responsibilities take up more time. Freelancing provides an opportunity to maintain the satisfaction of using a skill. Or perhaps an individual whose position does not currently permit use of the skills they enjoy most may freelance in that area until an improved regular employment opportunity presents itself.

Regardless of one's employment status, freelancing offers a chance to focus on the skill areas which an individual enjoys, or that he or she feels must be developed and polished to improve career advancement opportunities.

BUILDING A PORTFOLIO

Whether finding your first business communications job, or positioning yourself for that ideal career opening, building your professional skills, experience and reputation should be an ongoing process. Since you must "sell" yourself to potential employers, creating the ideal "package" of a business communicator with demonstrated skills and experience is a task requiring conscious attention.

Chapter 6 discussed the need to both create a portfolio of work samples and a resume demonstrating individual accomplishments and abilities. These are the sales tools that prove crucial in the search for employment in the field.

Employers look for *demonstrated* skills—the broader a base of skills the better. Communications managers especially are called upon to be versatile and competent in a wide variety of skills. Very frequently they will be much younger than the senior executives they work with—executives who have had many more years to gain their diversity of experience.

Freelancing is an excellent way to build a wide base of experience in a short time. Working as a freelancer in marketing communications can produce an impressive "client list" which demonstrates versatility and exposure to a wide range of business situations and communications challenges. Work with trade publications indicates a knowledge of specific industries which may significantly enhance employment opportunities. Professional contacts can be built which may lead to improved full time employment later. Freelancers are often hired as permanent employees, once they have demonstrated their ability and dependability.

Businesses always prefer to hire a known quantity rather than sift through stacks of resumes.

Communicators are fortunate in that freelancing provides an excellent opportunity to "flesh out" and polish their "sales tools", the resume and portfolio. Every resume should list "freelancing" under experience, with an accompanying list of publications and projects. The college student can build experience while still in school—and lack of experience is usually the single most significant deficiency in the new graduate's resume. Practicing communicators can demonstrate competency in areas in which their regular jobs do not allow them to work. And individuals contemplating a lateral move into the communications field can "test the water" by freelancing to explore personal aptitude for the work while improving their qualifications.

PUBLISHED WORK

A truism in the field is that "published impresses." Right or wrong, nothing seems to class up a portfolio or impress a potential employer more than published work. A byline in a newspaper or magazine works wonders. Just as it is human nature to find something more credible if printed, published work lends credibility and professionalism to portfolios and work samples. This is perhaps truer than it should be, for it only requires a reasonable level of competency and a certain amount of tenacity to become a published writer. While competition for space in the high-paying national publications is certainly keen, there are literally thousands of smaller circulation publications, many in desperate need of competently produced freelance work.

WRITING ABILITY

Writing ability is the basic, bottom-line, have-to-have skill for a business communicator. Without it, you should probably consider work in another area, or at least a serious effort to develop writing skills. Without tangible demonstrations of writing ability—printed pieces—you may experience difficulty in landing the position you want.

Not only that, but it's fun! Whether writing a magazine article, a story for the local newspaper, or copy for a brochure or advertisement, seeing your work in print produces a sense of satisfaction and accomplishment. This satisfaction and accomplishment can provide motivation and enthusiasm while your search for that "ideal job" goes on. Every piece you write, every bit of experience you accumulate, moves you closer to your goal.

GETTING STARTED

There are many excellent books which provide a step-by-step explanation of selecting story ideas, writing query letters, preparing manuscripts, or exploring opportunities in marketing support or technical writing. (Several are listed under Selected Reading in this book's appendix) While it is not difficult, there are details that will make your efforts more professional and likely to succeed. These are beyond the scope of this book. However, here are a few guidelines which will start you on your way to becoming a successful freelancer.

Editorial Freelancing

If you are a beginner, start small. Don't set your sights on one of the large national publications for your first try. Examine the needs of local publications first—newspapers, regional magazines, newsletters, and the in-house publications of large organizations. Look through a copy of *Writers' Market* (see Selected Readings) for trade or specialty publications covering fields where you already have experience or knowledge. Don't worry too much about payment; the goal is to break into print.

In most cases you'll be better off to send an editor a brief letter outlining your story ideas and offering to write an article. This will cut down on the number of time-consuming articles you'll write which never see print.

Be prepared for rejection. It's a part of the process and to be expected. All writers experience it. Many times an editor will not be able to use your idea or article for reasons which have nothing to do with how good it is. Perhaps they've already accepted a similar story, or did one recently. If one publication turns down an idea, see if you can re-work it and offer it to someone else.

Read publications closely to see what their needs are and how their stories are written. If you find a publication you feel is appropriate, write or call the editor and ask what types of materials they would be interested in. You may be surprised at how receptive editors can be.

Read, read; write, write. Be tenacious. In the end, if your goal is to become a successful business communicator, being able to attach "published author" to your resume will prove well worth the effort.

Marketing Communications

Marketing communications expertise may be your best opening into the industry or area of business communications in which your interest lies. Contacts from memberships in professional organizations are a good place to start. Let acquaintances who work as in-house communications staff know of your availability and areas of expertise. Many organizations' needs do not justify full-time communications experts, so they rely on outside help. Heavy workloads may also necessitate bringing in outside help.

Agencies involved in advertising, public relations, marketing and graphic design often use outside talent. For them this is a useful way to cut overhead by keeping the full-time staffs small. Send resumes to such agencies with a cover letter briefly describing your qualifications, background and experience, and availability for assignments. Enclose writing samples of previous work. Follow-up with a phone call to ask for an opportunity to visit in person and show your portfolio.

Technical Communications

Opportunities in technical communications are more specialized than other areas—by definition. There is a definite need and market for individuals who can understand technical subjects and write in a clear, comprehensible fashion. The task of these writers is to bridge the understanding gap between the technical (and often jargon-ridden) world of the technician and the more down-to-earth realm of the average individual.

This is not an easy task. The demand is there for those with the talent to achieve it, and as our society promises to become ever more technical, the demand will continue to rise. It is an area which offers the best prospects of steady freelance employment, because once relationships are established they tend to be maintained for long periods of time.

Building a portfolio of trade or specialty articles dealing with technical subjects is a good start in this area. These are your calling cards to send to those businesses which are identified as having technical writing needs. Again, your professional contacts can be of great assistance in locating appropriate businesses and getting a foot in the door.

Not-For-Profit Freelancing

There is something indisputably satisfying about being paid for your work. Right or wrong, we are part of a society where the "value" of our efforts is most often judged by what others are willing to pay for it.

Nonetheless, money is only one of the rewards of freelancing. For the freelancer interested in furthering a career it is probably the least important.

Recognizing this, the aspiring communicator should not disdain the many organizations which have a desperate need for communications help, and would welcome assistance with open arms. Most of the same benefits of paid freelancing may be gained by volunteer assistance to worthy community volunteer organizations. In fact, volunteering to chair a communications committee, or serve as a volunteer communications staff person, may give you a broader range of experience at a younger age then you could hope for in a regular business environment. The satisfaction of contributing to a worthy cause compensates in varying degrees for lack of monetary rewards.

Many prominent business leaders are involved in community volunteerism and active involvement is a time-honored means of making valuable personal contacts. A list of communications-related activities also demonstrates initiative, commitment to communications as a profession (you haven't just decided that this is what you want *this* week), and commitment to the local community.

Communicators often find community relations one of their responsibilities, and the ability to organize and work with volunteers is a valuable asset in the eyes of most employers. Volunteer communications work can also provide satisfaction and a feeling of progress when these are lacking in regular employment. Beginners in the field especially are likely to take a position that is less than ideal, at least initially, and volunteerism can keep the enthusiasm high while experience builds.

SUMMARY

Freelancing offers flexibility. It can be a part-time or full-time job. It can provide money, experience, satisfaction, and work samples which may lead to better employment.

Because freelancing can be done in addition to a regular position, it offers an opportunity to build experience and credentials necessary for improved employment, as well as providing a source of enthusiasm and motivation when current employment is less than satisfactory.

It also offers an excellent means for students to gain experience, the lack of which is so often a great obstacle to initial employment.

If you have focused your employment objective sufficiently, freelancing can help you achieve it. In some respects it is a benefit of working in the business communications field. Every communicator or would be communicator should consider freelancing, commensurate with her or his individual goals, resources and needs.

CHAPTER 10

THE FUTURE AND ETHICS

*To them, I said, the truth would be literally nothing
but the shadows of images.*

Plato
"The Parable of the Lights in the Cave"

In Plato's *Republic,* the Greek philosopher told a parable
of a cave in which several people were confined so as to be
able to see in only one direction. In this one direction was a
low wall, with a fire behind it, so that as people passed back
and forth behind this wall the prisoners could only see their
shadows.

If this were the case, Plato asked, would not the silhouettes
constitute what the prisoners considered to be "real?"
Wouldn't their "truth," he asked, "be literally nothing but
the shadows of images?"

EXPERIENCE, MEDIA, AND REALITY

In today's world, we personally experience only a tiny percentage of the events which affect our lives. Most events,
people, and organizations that we consider "real" are real to
us only on the basis of what others have communicated

about them. There is too much going on, too much information available, and not enough time for us to personally experience it all. We rely on others not only to inform us, but to interpret events, to tell us who people are, what they stand for, and what they mean when they talk. We rely on others to tell us about our world and how we should act if we want to conform to society's expectations.

We rely on the mass media—television, radio, newspapers, and magazines. We are also constantly bombarded with other messages—in advertising on billboards and bumper stickers, from corporate communications and from the government, and from the "junk mail" we find in our mail boxes. In a sense, we are a "captive" audience, relentlessly subjected to an intensifying assault of communications.

If we are at the mercy of others in shaping our perceptions of our world, could not our "reality" too become "nothing but the shadows of images?"

INFORMING TO INFLUENCE, OR BENDING THE TRUTH?

This portion of this book is admittedly somewhat self-serving. The communications process has always been susceptible to error and distortion at best and, at worst, outright manipulation. Admittedly, the professional communicator's concern is with influencing human behavior. We want consumers to buy our companies' products or services. All organizations want local communities to support their actions, to say good things about them, or perhaps merely to leave them alone in pursuing their preferred courses of action.

Where do you draw the line between informing to influence, and bending the truth to manipulate? The term "public relations" is tainted, perhaps irreversibly so, by its association with manipulation and "image building." We find little to praise in representing a person or organization as something more than what they actually are. There is a thin line indeed between putting your best foot forward, trying to get credit for your accomplishments and good works, and intentionally misleading people into thinking you are something other than what you really are.

The question of a communicator's commitment to truth is important, because the basis of a democratic society is the principle that—given full and accurate information—the individual is fully capable of making the best decisions on matters which affect her or his life. The quality and accuracy of information affects the quality of our decisions.

The ability to communicate is the ability to influence, and the ability to influence is power. This is a responsibility the professional communicator must be aware of. It is an ethical question. And, because the communicator works for others—whether management, a client, or simply "the boss"—how far should he or she go in directing the process to achieve the results which are demanded? Should our messages to employees, customers, and the community reflect reality as others see it, as we see it, or reality as we would like others to see it? Are we willing intentionally to mislead? Or are we simply "hired guns," who may rightfully leave these considerations to others?

Do we really serve our organizations by risking their credibility with distortions? Are we willing to stick with the truth, even at the cost of our jobs?

ARE THESE QUESTIONS RELEVANT?

Why ask these questions? Because it is better that you ask them of yourself now, rather than face them years down the road as a practicing communications professional. In what areas are you willing to compromise? How strong is your sense of integrity and honesty?

If the communications profession is to remain strong and prosper, it must have practitioners of integrity. In any communication process, credibility is absolutely essential. It is a state of mind which all organizations must maintain with their many "publics." It is difficult to achieve, and easy to lose.

To gain the prominence and respect which the profession deserves, it must have practitioners of conscience. It must have credibility with its audiences and within its own organizations. While it makes the job more difficult, ultimately this course best serves the practitioner, the organization, the public and society.

This is a challenge. One of many, true, but perhaps the most important of all.

Consider it closely in making your career decision. If you are comfortable with it, then join us as a professional communicator, and welcome.

We need you.

BIBLIOGRAPHY OF DIRECTORIES

Research is an essential part of both a successful career evaluation and a successful job search. The following directories can provide valuable assistance for either or both. Most of these directories will be available through local libraries. Purchase prices vary, but can be quite high.

ORGANIZATIONAL DIRECTORIES

Directory of Business and Organizational Communicators. Published annually by the International Association of Business Communicators as a service to members. The most recent issue lists more than 12,000 communications professionals in the United States, Canada, and 40 other countries. Listings are alphabetical, geographical, and by industry/organization. An invaluable resource for identifying both employment opportunities and potential contacts in the field. International Association of Business Communicators, 870 Market Street, Suite 940, San Francisco, California 94102.

The Encyclopedia of Associations. An extensive directory of more than 8,000 national trade, business, professional, hobby and special interest organizations. Categorized by subject, title, keyword or geographic location. Provides names, addresses, telephone numbers, staff and membership size, principal activities and publications. Published by the Gale Research Company.

National Trade & Professional Associations Directory. A directory of more than 7,000 national trade associations, labor unions, professional, scientific or technical societies and other national organizations composed of groups united for a common purpose. Provides information on location, purpose, budget, staff size, and publications. Published by Columbia Books, Inc., 1350 New York Avenue, N.W., Suite 207, Washington, D.C. 20005.

PUBLICATION DIRECTORIES

Ulrich's International Periodicals Directory. A listing of more than 66,000 magazines, journals, and other serials in 557 subjects, worldwide. Provides location of publication, circulation, and publisher. Published by the R. R. Bowker Company.

The Internal Publications Directory. A directory of 3,500 in-house publications and the organizations which publish them. An excellent guide to organizations with significant communications programs. The Working Press of the Nation, National Research Bureau, 310 South Michigan Avenue, Chicago, Illinois 60604.

Writer's Market. A popular directory of book and magazine publishers used widely by freelance writers. Available at most book stores at a reasonable price. Lists magazines and trade publications by subject category. Provides information on content, circulation, payment rates for freelance work, topics of particular interest to the publication, and hints on working with editors. Writer's Digest Books, 9933 Alliance Road, Cincinnati, Ohio 45242.

IMS/Ayer Directory of Publications. A comprehensive reference guide to newspapers, magazines, journals and newsletters published in the United States, Canada, Puerto Rico, Virgin Islands, Bahamas, Bermuda and the Republic of the Philippines. Published annually since 1869. Provides mailing addresses, phone numbers, circulation, editor's name, and population of community in which published. IMS Press, A Division of IMS Communications, Inc., 426 Pennsylvania Avenue, Fort Washington, Pennsylvania 19034.

GOVERNMENT PUBLICATIONS

Occupational Outlook Handbook. Published by the U.S. Department of Labor, this publication provides long-term forecasts for skills demand, a review of education and training requirements, duties and working conditions and average earnings. Provides sources of further information for many occupational entries.

Dictionary of Occupational Titles. A comprehensive directory of job titles and brief job descriptions published by the federal government. A good tool for familiarizing oneself with various job titles associated with the communications field.

U.S. Government Organization Manual. An excellent information source for positions within the federal government. This publication describes work, responsibilities and authority of all federal agencies and lists office locations. Provides insight into state and local government agency structures as well, most of which are patterned after federal plans.

MISCELLANEOUS

Dun and Bradstreet Directories. Dun and Bradstreet's *Billion Dollar* and *Million Dollar* directories together comprise the largest general business directory available. The *Billion Dollar Directory* lists 2,500 parent companies and 28,000 subsidiaries, providing addresses, financial data, officer's names, and staff size.

The Directory of Directories. Published by the Gale Research Company, a directory of directories. Organized by subjects, with multiple indexes. More than 7,000 entries for directories of domestic, foreign and international coverage.

EXAMPLES OF EXECUTIVE SEARCH FIRMS SPECIALIZING IN PUBLIC RELATIONS AND BUSINESS COMMUNICATIONS

The Cantor Concern
39 West 55 Street
New York, NY 10019
(212) 246-2700

Howard/Sloan Associates, Inc.
545 Fifth Avenue
New York, NY 10017
(212) 661-5250

Marshall Consultants, Inc.
360 East 65th Street
New York, NY 10021

Placement Associates, Inc.
80 Fifth Avenue
New York, NY 10011
(212) 620-7620

Toby Clark Associates, Inc.
155 E. 55 Street
New York, NY 10022
(212) 752-5670*

---

*These organizations advertise as specializing in the communications field. No endorsement or guarantee of their services is implied. You will want to research the telephone Yellow Pages and other sources in your locale, for additional examples.

SAMPLE RESUME: ENTRY LEVEL

Lee L. Smith
2010 West Street
Sacramento, California 99999
(916) 555-5555

OBJECTIVE

A responsible career position with a public relations agency where education and related experience can be effectively used.

EDUCATION

Bachelor of Arts, Journalism, 1985
California State University, Chico
Minor: Public Relations
G.P.A. – 3.45

Associate of Arts, 1982
Sierra Junior College
Rocklin, California

SUMMARY OF EXPERIENCE

JOURNALISM—Reporter for The Orion, campus weekly newspaper, 1984. Bylined contributions to the Carmichael Times. Freelance article published in Sacramento magazine.

COMMUNICATIONS—Internship with Old Sacramento Citizens and

Merchants Association. Served as Public Relations Assistant for two semesters. Developed news releases and assisted in coordination of special events.

ADVERTISING—Organized a promotional logo, and slogan design contents for Gold's Travel Agency.

UNIVERSITY ACTIVITIES

Member, Student Chapter, International Association of Business Communicators.

Publicity Director, KLAX, campus radio station.

President, Chi Omega sorority, 1984.

Publicity coordinator, University Y.M.C.A.

REFERENCES

Available upon request.

SAMPLE RESUME: ADVANCED

Ray E. Jones
4200 S. Camino Real
Oceanside, California 99999
(714) 555-5555

CAREER OBJECTIVE

To direct marketing efforts for health care products or services.

QUALIFIED BY

More than 10 years' experience in marketing, including 8 in the health care industry.

EXPERIENCE

1981–present—Coronado Health Corporation, Director of Community Relations.

Responsible for the operations of the Community Relations Department of the Community Services Division of one of Southern California's largest vertically-oriented health care organizations. Responsibilities include the research, planning and implementation of all division marketing activities. Business plan-based marketing activities include advertising campaigns, media relations and publications for new and existing services/programs, as well as for educational conferences. Also act as advisor for corporate marketing planning and facilitate interdivisional communication.

1978–1981: Hospital Respiratory Services, Director of Marketing and Public Relations.

Responsible for the development of a new subsidiary for a corporation which owned and managed hospitals in the Western United States. Assessed, placed and managed independent respiratory service departments in Southern California community hospitals. Conducted feasibility studies to determine appropriate placement and then directed department managers in marketing efforts via physician contact, community presentations, and in-hospital communications.

January–June, 1978: Phil Landers for Congress Committee, Press Secretary.

Responsible for the media relations and advertising strategies during Congressman's first primary campaign.

1977–1978: School of Medicine, University of Southern California, Director, Impact of Hypertension Information Study.

Responsible for coordinating the West Coast segment of a National Institute of Health study. Assisted in development of national survey instrument, marketed to designated populations, trained and supervised staff of 35, and presented data for analysis according to stringent research requirements.

1974–1977: Imperial Girl Scout Council, Field Director.

Marketed Girl Scout programs in San Diego County. Responsible for recruiting girls and adults via targeted marketing activities, including advertising, public presentations, community and media relations, and direct mail.

EDUCATION

Bachelor of Arts, Behavior Science, San Diego State University.

PROFESSIONAL AFFILIATIONS

San Diego Health Consortium 1981–85; President 1985 International Association of Business Communicators V.P.; Professional Development, 1984 North San Diego County Marketing Association 1982–85

COMMUNITY AFFILIATIONS

Cerebral Palsy Association
Coronado Boy Scout Council
Junior League of San Diego
United Way, San Diego

REFERENCES

Available upon request

SAMPLE WRITING ADDENDUM

Fred Jones
999 Sanford Ave.
Indianapolis, Indiana 46220
(317) 257-2134

WRITING ADDENDUM

Editorial/Newswriting

"If You Can't Beat 'Em Join 'Em," Modern Brewery Age, July 1985.

"Deep Pockets," Indiana Journal of State Government, December 1984.

"When TV Calls," Better Communication, No. 343, September 1985.

"The Staggering Cost of Health Care Benefits," Business Managers Weekly, March 13 issue, 1985.

Marketing

Direct mail pieces—Northland Electric Supply Co. (new product introduction), Mercy House Center for Children (fundraiser), Bill Wilson for City Council (political). Advertising—Northland Electric; Indiana Softdrinks, Inc.; Bowling Association of Wisconsin; Midwest Business Machines. Brochures—Conreal Development, Big Eddy's Gourmet Hamburger Joint, Western Women in Real Estate, Donnejohn's Department Stores.

Technical Writing

User manual for System for Wholesale Distributors software package, Data American Corporation. Article "Finding the Right Spread Sheet" for Today's Personal Computer, August 85 issue.

Public Relations

News releases for American Cancer Society annual awards program, United Way 1984 campaign, Northland Electric Supply new product introduction (trade publications), and feature articles on the "Big Eddy's Gourmet Hamburger."

THESE ARE REPRESENTATIVE SAMPLES. COPIES OF THESE AND OTHER WRITING SAMPLES ARE AVAILABLE UPON REQUEST.

SAMPLE COVER LETTER

June 12, 198_

Mr. John Winston
Communications Director
Daytron, Inc.
4444 Airport Road
Phoenix, Arizona 99999

Dear Mr. Winston:

I understand from your marketing director, Susan Thompson, that you are currently seeking an assistant editor for your publication, Daytron Today, and I would appreciate being considered for the position.

My experience and educational background—outlined in the enclosed resume—have been specifically tailored with just such a position in mind. I am confident I would be able to step right in and immediately be an asset to you.

Daytron Today's tabloid format is quite similar to the CSU Chico Orion, where I worked two years as a writer and editor. And with Daytron's operations so diverse and widespread, you'll want someone who can operate independently—visiting various locations to research and write feature stories. You'll note from the enclosed writing addendum that I have a demonstrated ability to successfully accomplish these types of assignments.

Your company is quite attractive to me as a potential employer, and I would welcome an opportunity to discuss further how I might assist you in meeting your business objectives.

I will call next week to gauge your interest and see if there would be a convenient time for us to meet.

Sincerely,

Jane Smith

Encl: Resume
       Writing addendum

APPENDIX G

BIBLIOGRAPHY OF SELECTED RELATED READING

BOOKS

Barban, Arnold M.; Cristol, Steven M.; Kopec, Frank J. *Essentials of Media Planning.* 2nd ed. Lincolnwood, Illinois: NTC Business Books, 1986.

Beach, Mark. *Editing Your Newsletter.* Portland, Oregon: Coast to Coast Books, 1982.

Biagi, Shirley. *How to Write and Sell Magazine Articles.* New York, Spectrum Books, Prentice-Hall, Inc., 1983.

Brennan, John F., Jr. *The Conscious Communicator.* Reading, Massachusetts: Addison-Wesley, 1974.

Dartnell Public Relations Handbook, Chicago: Dartnell, 1980.

Detz, Joan. *How to Write & Give a Speech.* New York: St. Martins Press, 1984.

Foote-Smith, Elizabeth. *Opportunities in Writing Careers.* Lincolnwood, Illinois: VGM Career Horizons, National Textbook Company, 1985.

Gould, Jay; Losano, Wayne. *Opportunities in Technical Communications.* Lincolnwood, Illinois: VGM Career Horizons, National Textbook Co., 1984.

Grunig, James E., and Hunt, Todd. *Managing Public Relations.* New York: Holt, Rinehart and Winston, 1984.

Hennessey, Bernard C. *Public Opinion.* Belmont, California: Wadsworth Publishing Company.

133

Higgins, Denis. *The Art of Writing Advertising.* Lincolnwood, Illinois: NTC Business Books, 1986.

Inside Organizational Communication. Reuss, Carol; Silvis, Don, eds. International Association of Business Communicators. Longman, New York & London, 1985.

Katz, Daniel, and Kahn, Robert L. *The Social Psychology of Organizations.* New York: John Wiley & Sons.

Mathieu, Aron. *The Creative Writer.* Revised edition, Cincinnati: Writer's Digest Books.

Mau, Ernest E. *The Freelance Writers Survival Manual.* Chicago: Contemporary Books, Inc.

Meltzler, Ken. *Creative Interviewing.* Englewood Cliffs, N.J.: Prentice-Hall, 1977.

Nager, Norman R., and Allen, Harrell T. *Public Relations Management by Objective.* New York: Longman, 1983.

Noronha, Shonan. *Careers in Communications.* Lincolnwood, Illinois: VGM Career Horizons, National Textbook Co., 1987.

Newsom, Douglas Ann, and Scott, Alan. *This is PR: Realities of Public Relations.* Belmont, California: Wadsworth, 1981.

Nolte, Lawrence, and Wilcox, Dennis. *Effective Publicity.* Columbus: Grid Inc., 1984.

Palmer, W.R. *Freelance Business—Writing Business.* Monmouth Junction, New Jersey: Heathcote Publishers.

Pattis, S. William. *Opportunities in Advertising Careers.* Lincolnwood, Illinois: VGM Career Horizons, National Textbook Co., 1985.

Rivers, William L.; Smolkin, Shelley. *Free-Lancer and Staff Writer,* 3rd ed. Belmont, California: Wadsworth, 1980.

Robinson, William A. *Best Sales Promotion.* 6th ed. Lincolnwood, Illinois: NTC Business Books, 1986.

Rogers, Everett M.; Agarwala-Rogers, Rehka. *Communication in Organizations,* 4th ed. New York: Free Press (Macmillan), 1976.

Roman, Kenneth; Raphaelson, Joel. *Writing that Works.* New York: Harper & Row, 1981.

Ross, Robert D. *Management of Public Relations.* New York: Wiley, 1978.

Rotman, Morris B. *Opportunities in Public Relations Careers.* Lincolnwood, Illinois: VGM Career Horizons, National Textbook Company, 1985.

Simon, Raymond. *Publicity and Public Relations Worktext.* 5th Ed. Columbus: Grid Inc., 1983.

Turnbull, Arthur T., and Baird, Russell N. *The Graphics of Communication.* New York: Holt, Rinehart and Winston, 1980.

Walsh, Frank,. *The PR Writer.* Englewood Cliffs, New Jersey: Prentice Hall, 1983.

Wells, Theodora. *Keeping Your Cool Under Fire: Communicating Non-Defensively.* New York: McGraw-Hill, 1979.

Writer's Market. Writer's Digest Books. Cincinnati, Ohio.

Zand, Dale E. *Information, Organization, and Power: Effective Management in the Knowledge Society.* New York: McGraw-Hill, 1981.

Zinsser, William. *On Writing Well.* 2nd ed. New York: Harper & Row, 1980.

PROFESSIONAL JOURNALS AND PERIODICAL PUBLICATIONS OF INTEREST TO COMMUNICATORS

AdWeek/West. A weekly magazine for "people involved in advertising: media, agencies, and client organizations as well as affiliated businesses." 415 Shatto Place, Los Angeles, CA, 90020.

Communication Arts. A bimonthly magazine for designers. 410 Sherman Avenue, Palo Alto, CA, 94303.

Communication Briefings. A monthly newsletter which "provides subscribers with down-to-earth communication ideas and techniques." 806 Westminster Blvd., Blackwood NJ, 08012.

Communication Illustrated. A monthly newsletter of ideas, techniques and strategies for business communicators. P.O. Box 924, Bartlesville, OK, 74005.

Communication World. Monthly publication of the International Association of Business Communicators. "Published to provide information about the profession of organizational communication and news of IABC, its members, chapters, districts and international affiliates. IABC, 870 Market Street, Suite 940, San Francisco, CA, 94102.

Editor & Publisher. A monthly publication primarily for members of the newspaper industry. Carries classified advertisements for editorial, public relations, and teaching positions. 575 Lexington Ave., New York, NY, 10022.

Editors Forum. A monthly newsletter for newsletter editors. P.O. Box 1806, Kansas City, MO, 64141.

Public Relations Journal. Monthly magazine of the Public Relations Society of America. 845 Third Avenue, New York, NY, 10022.

PR News. A four-page weekly newsletter for those in public relations. 127 East 89th St., New York, NY, 10021.

Writer's Digest. A monthly magazine about writing and publishing, very useful to freelance writers. From the publishers of Writer's Market. 9933 Alliance Rd., Cincinnati, OH, 45242.

APPENDIX H

THE IABC CODE OF ETHICS*

The IABC Code of Ethics has been developed to provide IABC members and other communication professionals with guidelines of professional behavior and standards of ethical practice. The Code is reviewed and revised as necessary by the Ethics Committee and the Executive Board.

Any IABC member who wishes advice and guidance regarding its interpretation and/or application may write or phone IABC headquarters. Questions will be routed to the Executive Board member responsible for the Code.

COMMUNICATION AND INFORMATION DISSEMINATION

---

1. Communication professionals will uphold the credibility and dignity of their profession by encouraging the practice of honest, candid and timely communication.

---

*Reprinted with permission of the International Association of Business Communicators.

The highest standards of professionalism will be upheld in all communication. Communicators should encourage frequent communication and messages that are honest in their content, candid, accurate and appropriate to the needs of the organization and its audiences.

2. *Professional communicators will not use any information that has been generated or appropriately acquired by a business for another business without permission. Further, communicators should attempt to identify the source of information to be used.*

When one is changing employers, information developed at the previous position will not be used without permission from that employer. Acts of plagiarism and copyright infringement are illegal acts; material in the public domain should have its source attributed, if possible. If an organization grants permission to use its information and requests public acknowledgement, it will be made in a place appropriate to the material used. The material will be used only for the purpose for which permission was granted.

STANDARDS OF CONDUCT

3. *Communication professionals will abide by the spirit and letter of all laws and regulations governing their professional activities.*

All international, national and local laws and regulations must be observed, with particular attention to those pertaining to communication, such as copyright law. Industry and organizational regulations will also be observed.

4. *Communication professionals will not condone any illegal or unethical act related to their professional activity, their organization and its business or the public environment in which it operates.*

It is the personal responsibility of professional communicators to act honestly, fairly and with integrity at all times in all professional activities. Looking the other way while others act illegally tacitly condones such acts whether or not the communicator has commited them. The communicator should speak with the individual involved, his or her supervisor or appropriate authorities—depending on the context of the situation and one's own ethical judgment.

CONFIDENTIALITY/DISCLOSURE

5. *Communication professionals will respect the confidentiality and right-to-privacy of all individuals, employers, clients and customers.*

Communicators must determine the ethical balance between right-to-privacy and need-to-know. Unless the situation involves illegal or grossly unethical acts, confidences should be maintained. If there is a conflict between right-to-privacy and need-to-know, a communicator should first talk with the source and negotiate the need for the information to be communicated.

6. *Communication professionals will not use any confidential information gained as a result of professional activity for personal benefit or for that of others.*

Confidential information can be used to give inside advantage to stock transactions, gain favors from outsiders, assist a competing company for whom one is going to work, assist companies in developing a marketing advantage, achieve a publishing advantage or otherwise act to the detriment of an organization. Such information must remain confidential during and after one's employment period.

PROFESSIONALISM

7. *Communication professionals should uphold IABC's standards for ethical conduct in all professional activity, and should use IABC and its designation of accreditation (ABC) only for purposes that are authorized and fairly represent the organization and its professional standards.*

IABC recognizes the need for professional integrity within any organization, including the association. Members should acknowledge that their actions reflect on themselves, their organizations and their profession.

VGM CAREER BOOKS

OPPORTUNITIES IN

*Available in both
paperback and hardbound
editions*

Accounting Careers
Acting Careers
Advertising Careers
Airline Careers
Animal and Pet Care
Appraising Valuation Science
Architecture
Automotive Service
Banking
Beauty Culture
Biological Sciences
Book Publishing Careers
Broadcasting Careers
Building Construction Trades
Business Communication Careers
Business Management
Cable Television
Carpentry Careers
Chemical Engineering
Chemistry Careers
Child Care Careers
Chiropractic Health Care
Civil Engineering
Commercial Art and Graphic
 Design
Computer Aided Design
 and Computer Aided Mfg.
Computer Science Careers
Counseling & Development
Dance
Data Processing Careers
Dental Care
Drafting Careers
Electrical Trades
Electronic and Electrical
 Engineering
Energy Careers
Engineering Technology
Environmental Careers
Fashion Careers
Federal Government Careers
Film Careers
Financial Careers
Fire Protection Services
Fitness Careers
Food Services
Foreign Language Careers
Forestry Careers

Free Lance Writing
Gerontology Careers
Government Service
Graphic Communications
Health and
 Medical Careers
Hospital Administration
Hotel & Motel Management
Industrial Design
Interior Design
Journalism Careers
Landscape Architecture
Law Careers
Law Enforcement and
 Criminal Justice
Library and Information
 Science
Machine Trades
Magazine Publishing Careers
Management
Marine & Maritime
Materials Science
Mechanical Engineering
Microelectronics
Modeling Careers
Music Careers
Nursing Careers
Nutrition Careers
Occupational Therapy
Office Occupations
Opticianry
Optometry
Packaging Science
Paralegal Careers
Paramedical Careers
Personnel Management
Pharmacy Careers
Photography
Physical Therapy Careers
Podiatric Medicine
Printing Careers
Psychiatry
Psychology
Public Relations Careers
Real Estate
Recreation and Leisure
Refrigeration and
 Air Conditioning
Religious Service
Sales & Marketing
Secretarial Careers
Securities Industry

Sports & Athletics
Sports Medicine
State and Local Government
Teaching Careers
Technical Communications
Telecommunications
Theatrical Design
 & Production
Transportation
Travel Careers
Veterinary Medicine
Word Processing
Writing Careers
Your Own Service Business

WOMEN IN

*Available in both
paperback and hardbound
editions*

Communications
Engineering
Finance
Government
Management
Science
Their Own Business

CAREER PLANNING

How to Get People to Do
 Things Your Way
How to Have a Winning
 Job Interview
How to Land a Better Job
How to Write a Winning
 Résumé
Life Plan
Planning Your Career Change
Planning Your Career of
 Tomorrow
Planning Your College
 Education
Planning Your Military Career
Planning Your Own Home
 Business
Planning Your Young Child's
 Education

SURVIVAL GUIDES

High School Survival Guide
College Survival Guide

VGM Career Horizons

A Division of National Textbook Company
4255 West Touhy Avenue
Lincolnwood, Illinois 60646-1975 U.S.A.